Cram101 Textbook Outlines to accompany:

Developing Management Skills

Whetten and Cameron, 5th Edition

An Academic Internet Publishers (AIPI) publication (c) 2007.

Cram101 and Cram101.com are AIPI publications and services. All notes, highlights, reviews, and practice tests are prepared by AIPI for use in AIPI publications, all rights reserved.

You have a discounted membership at www.Cram101.com with this book.

Get all of the practice tests for the chapters of this textbook, and access in-depth reference material for writing essays and papers. Here is an example from a Cram101 Biology text:

When you need problem solving help with math, stats, and other disciplines, www.Cram101.com will walk through the formulas and solutions step by step.

With Cram101.com online, you also have access to extensive reference material.

You will nail those essays and papers. Here is an example from a Cram101 Biology text:

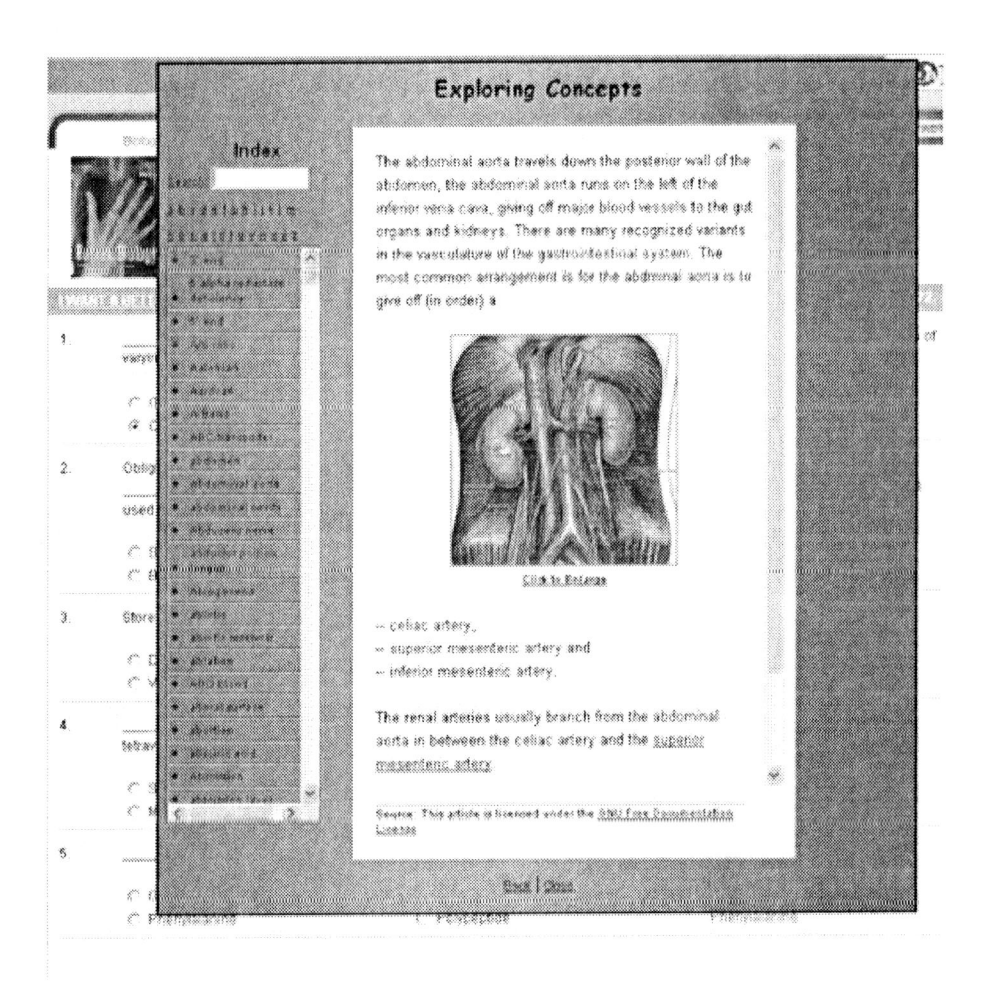

Visit **www.Cram101.com**, click Sign Up at the top of the screen, and enter DK73DW in the promo code box on the registration screen. Access to www.Cram101.com is normally $9.95, but because you have purchased this book, your access fee is only $4.95. Sign up and stop highlighting textbooks forever.

Learning System

Cram101 Textbook Outlines is a learning system. The notes in this book are the highlights of your textbook, you will never have to highlight a book again.

How to use this book. Take this book to class, it is your notebook for the lecture. The notes and highlights on the left hand side of the pages follow the outline and order of the textbook. All you have to do is follow along while your intructor presents the lecture. Circle the items emphasized in class and add other important information on the right side. With Cram101 Textbook Outlines you'll spend less time writing and more time listening. Learning becomes more efficient.

Cram101.com Online

Increase your studying efficiency by using Cram101.com's practice tests and online reference material. It is the perfect complement to Cram101 Textbook Outlines. Use self-teaching matching tests or simulate in-class testing with comprehensive multiple choice tests, or simply use Cram's true and false tests for quick review. Cram101.com even allows you to enter your in-class notes for an integrated studying format combining the textbook notes with your class notes.

Visit **www.Cram101.com**, click Sign Up at the top of the screen, and enter **DK73DW361** in the promo code box on the registration screen. Access to www.Cram101.com is normally $9.95, but because you have purchased this book, your access fee is only $4.95. Sign up and stop highlighting textbooks forever.

Copyright © 2007 by Academic Internet Publishers, Inc. All rights reserved. "Cram101"® and "Never Highlight a Book Again!"® are registered trademarks of Academic Internet Publishers, Inc. The Cram101 Textbook Outline series is printed in the United States. ISBN: 1-4288-0511-7

Developing Management Skills
Whetten and Cameron, 5th

CONTENTS

1. DEVELOPING SELF-AWARENESS 2
2. MANAGING PERSONAL STRESS 10
3. SOLVING PROBLEMS ANALYTICALLY AND CREATIVELY 18
4. COACHING, COUNSELING, AND SUPPORTIVE COMMUNICATION 26
5. GAINING POWER AND INFLUENCE 32
6. MOTIVATING OTHERS 44
7. MANAGING CONFLICT 56
8. EMPOWERING AND DELEGATING 68
9. BUILDING EFFECTIVE TEAMS AND TEAMWORK 76

Chapter 1. DEVELOPING SELF-AWARENESS

Dictum	Dictum refers to language in a judicial opinion that is not necessary for the decision of the case and that, while perhaps persuasive, does not bind subsequent courts.
Accounting	The recording, classifying, summarizing, and interpreting of financial events and transactions to provide management and other interested parties the information they need to make good decisions is called accounting.
Emotional intelligence	The ability to understand one's own emotions and the emotions of people with whom one interacts on a daily basis is referred to as the emotional intelligence.
Manager	A person who is formally responsible for supporting the work efforts of other people is a manager.
Competencies	An organization's special capabilities, including skills, technologies, and resources that distinguish it from other organizations are competencies.
Management	Management characterizes the process of leading and directing all or part of an organization, often a business, through the deployment and manipulation of resources. Early twentieth-century management writer Mary Parker Follett defined management as "the art of getting things done through people."
Assessment	Collecting information and providing feedback to employees about their behavior, communication style, or skills is an assessment.
Acceptance	The actual or implied receipt and retention of that which is tendered or offered is the acceptance.
Brief	Brief refers to a statement of a party's case or legal arguments, usually prepared by an attorney. Also used to make legal arguments before appellate courts.
Managing diversity	Building systems and a climate that unite different people in a common pursuit without undermining their individual strengths is managing diversity.
Charisma	A form of interpersonal attraction that inspires support and acceptance from others is charisma. It refers especially to a quality in certain people who easily draw the attention and admiration (or even hatred if the charisma is negative) of others due to a "magnetic" quality of personality and/or appearance.
Effective manager	Leader of a team that consistently achieves high performance goals is an effective manager.
Authority	Authority in agency law, refers to an agent's ability to affect his principal's legal relations with third parties. Also used to refer to an actor's legal power or ability to do something. In addition, sometimes used to refer to a statute, case, or other legal source that justifies a particular result.
Composition	An out-of-court settlement in which creditors agree to accept a fractional settlement on their original claim is referred to as composition.
Discount	A discount is the reduction of the base price of a product.
Marketing	The American Marketing Association suggests that Marketing is "the process of planning and executing the pricing, promotion, and distribution of goods, ideas, and services to create exchanges that satisfy individual and organizational goals."
Trust	Trust refers to a legal relationship in which a person who has legal title to property has the duty to hold it for the use or benefit of another person. The term is also used in a general sense to mean confidence reposed in one person by another.
Communication	Communication refers to the social process in which two or more parties exchange information and share meaning.
Empowerment	Giving employees the authority and responsibility to respond quickly to customer requests is called empowerment.
Controlling	A management function that involves determining whether or not an organization is progressing toward

Chapter 1. DEVELOPING SELF-AWARENESS

Chapter 1. DEVELOPING SELF-AWARENESS

	its goals and objectives, and taking corrective action if it is not is called controlling.
Inventory	Inventory refers to physical material purchased from suppliers, which may or may not be reworked for sale to customers. A unique element of services-the need for and cost of having a service provider available.
Myers-Briggs type indicator	Myers-Briggs type indicator refers to a psychological test used for team building and leadership development that identifies employees training needs by reviewing work tasks, identifying performance factors and objectives, and defining training objectives and recommendations.
Product	Any physical good, service, or idea that satisfies a want or need is called product. Product in project management is a physical entity created as a result of project work.
Contribution	In business organization law, the cash or property contributed to a business by its owners is referred to as contribution.
Negotiation	Negotiation is the process whereby interested parties resolve disputes, agree upon courses of action, bargain for individual or collective advantage, and/or attempt to craft outcomes which serve their mutual interests.
Loyalty	Marketers tend to define customer loyalty as making repeat purchases. Some argue that it should be defined attitudinally as a strongly positive feeling about the brand.
Organizational culture	Widely shared values within an organization that provide coherence and cooperation to achieve common goals are referred to as a organizational culture.
Holding	The holding is a court's determination of a matter of law based on the issue presented in the particular case. In other words: under this law, with these facts, this result.
Compatibility	Compatibility refers to used to describe a product characteristic, it means a good fit with other products used by the consumer or with the consumer's lifestyle. Used in a technical context, it means the ability of systems to work together.
Instrumental value	A values that reflects a person's beliefs about the means for achieving desired ends is referred to as an instrumental value.
Terminal value	In finance, the terminal value of a security is the present value at a future point in time of all future cash flows. It is most often used in multi-stage discounted cash flow analysis, and allows for the limitation of cash flow projections to a several-year period.
Cultural values	The values that employees need to have and act on for the organization to act on the strategic values are called cultural values.
Self-direction	A term that refers to providing autonomy to employees in terms of facilitating their own training needs is called self-direction.
Promotion	Promotion refers to all the techniques sellers use to motivate people to buy products or services. An attempt by marketers to inform people about products and to persuade them to participate in an exchange.
Comprehensive	A comprehensive refers to a layout accurate in size, color, scheme, and other necessary details to show how a final ad will look. For presentation only, never for reproduction.
Property	Property refers to something that is capable of being owned. A right or interest associated with something that gives the owner the ability to exercise dominion over it.
Equity	Equity is the name given to the set of legal principles, in countries following the English common law tradition, which supplement strict rules of law where their application would operate harshly, so as to achieve what is sometimes referred to as "natural justice."
Insurance	A means for persons and businesses to protect themselves against the risk of loss is insurance.

Chapter 1. DEVELOPING SELF-AWARENESS

Chapter 1. DEVELOPING SELF-AWARENESS

Principal	In agency law, one under whose direction an agent acts and for whose benefit that agent acts is a principal.
Compromise	Compromise occurs when the interaction is moderately important to meeting goals and the goals are neither completely compatible nor completely incompatible.
Competitive advantage	A business is said to have a competitive advantage when its unique strengths, often based on cost, quality, time, and innovation, offer consumers a greater percieved value and there by differtiating it from its competitors.
Tangible	Having a physical existence is referred to as the tangible. Personal property other than real estate, such as cars, boats, stocks, or other assets.
Utility	An economic term that refers to the value or want-satisfying ability that's added to goods or services by organizations when the products are made more useful or accessible to consumers than before is a utility.
Kite	Kite refers to a bank check that has been fraudulently altered to increase its face value.
Preference	The act of a debtor in paying or securing one or more of his creditors in a manner more favorable to them than to other creditors or to the exclusion of such other creditors is a preference. In the absence of statute, a preference is perfectly good, but to be legal it must be bona fide, and not a mere subterfuge of the debtor to secure a future benefit to himself or to prevent the application of his property to his debts.
Idea generation	Developing a pool of concepts as candidates for new products is called idea generation.
Brainstorming	Brainstorming refers to a technique designed to overcome our natural tendency to evaluate and criticize ideas and thereby reduce the creative output of those ideas. People are encouraged to produce ideas/options without criticizing, often at a very fast pace to minimize our natural tendency to criticize.
Public policy	Decision making by government. Governments are constantly concerned about what they should or should not do. And whatever they do or do not do is public policy. public program All those activities designed to implement a public policy; often this calls for the creation of organizations, public agencies, and bureaus.
Policy	Similar to a script in that a policy can be a less than completely rational decision-making method. Involves the use of a pre-existing set of decision steps for any problem that presents itself.
Economics	The study of how society chooses to employ resources to produce goods and services and distribute them for consumption among various competing groups and individuals is economics.
Administration	Administration refers to the management and direction of the affairs of governments and institutions; a collective term for all policymaking officials of a government; the execution and implementation of public policy.
Confirmed	When the seller's bank agrees to assume liability on the letter of credit issued by the buyer's bank the transaction is confirmed. The term means that the credit is not only backed up by the issuing foreign bank, but that payment is also guaranteed by the notifying American bank.
Forming	The first stage of team development, where the team is formed and the objectives for the team are set is referred to as forming.
Exhibit	Exhibit refers to a copy of a written instrument on which a pleading is founded, annexed to the pleading and by reference made a part of it. Any paper or thing offered in evidence and marked for identification.
Case study	A case study is a particular method of qualitative research. Rather than using large samples and following a rigid protocol to examine a limited number of variables, case study methods involve an in-depth, longitudinal examination of a single instance or event: a case. They provide a systematic way of

Go to **Cram101.com** for the Practice Tests for this Chapter.

Chapter 1. DEVELOPING SELF-AWARENESS

Chapter 1. DEVELOPING SELF-AWARENESS

	looking at events, collecting data, analyzing information, and reporting the results.
Action learning	Action learning refers to teams working on an actual business problem, commiting to an action plan, and are accountable for carrying out the plan.
Channel	Channel, in communications (sometimes called communications channel), refers to the medium used to convey information from a sender (or transmitter) to a receiver.
Information technology	Information technology refers to technology that helps companies change business by allowing them to use new methods.
Status quo	The existing state of things is the status quo. In contract law, returning a party to status quo or status quo ante means putting him in the position he was in before entering the contract.
E-business	E-business refers to work an organization does using electronic linkages; any business that takes place by digital processes over a computer network rather than in a physical space.
Competitor	Other organizations in the same industry or type of business that provide a good or service to the same set of customers is referred to as a competitor.
Complexity	The technical sophistication of the product and hence the amount of understanding required to use it is referred to as complexity. It is the opposite of simplicity.
Aptitude	An aptitude is an innate inborn ability to do a certain kind of work. Aptitudes may be physical or mental. Many of them have been identified and are testable.
Downsizing	The process of eliminating managerial and non-managerial positions are called downsizing.
Evaluation	The consumer's appraisal of the product or brand on important attributes is called evaluation.
External locus of control	The belief by individuals that their future is not within their control but rather is influenced by external forces is referred to as external locus of control.
Coercive power	Coercive power refers to the extent to which a person has the ability to punish or physically or psychologically harm someone else.
Innovation	The process of creating and doing new things that are introduced into the marketplace as products, processes, or services is innovation.
Authoritarianism	The belief that power and status differences are appropriate within hierarchical social systems such as organizations is referred to as authoritarianism.
Small business	Small business refers to a business that is independently owned and operated, is not dominant in its field of operation, and meets certain standards of size in terms of employees or annual receipts.
Teamwork	That which occurs when group members work together in ways that utilize their skills well to accomplish a purpose is called teamwork.

Chapter 1. DEVELOPING SELF-AWARENESS

Chapter 2. MANAGING PERSONAL STRESS

Management	Management characterizes the process of leading and directing all or part of an organization, often a business, through the deployment and manipulation of resources. Early twentieth-century management writer Mary Parker Follett defined management as "the art of getting things done through people."
Economy	The income, expenditures, and resources that affect the cost of running a business and household are called an economy.
Corporation	A form of business organization that is owned by owners, called shareholders, who have no inherent right to manage the business, and is managed by a board of directors that is elected by the shareholders is called a corporation.
Compensation	A payment that is given or recieved as reparation for a service or loss is referred to as compensation.
Manager	A person who is formally responsible for supporting the work efforts of other people is a manager.
Product	Any physical good, service, or idea that satisfies a want or need is called product. Product in project management is a physical entity created as a result of project work.
Brief	Brief refers to a statement of a party's case or legal arguments, usually prepared by an attorney. Also used to make legal arguments before appellate courts.
Adoption	In corporation law, a corporation's acceptance of a pre-incorporation contract by action of its board of directors, by which the corporation becomes liable on the contract, is referred to as adoption.
Dissolution	Dissolution is the process of admitting or removing a partner in a partnership.
Proactive strategies	New product strategies that involve an aggressive allocation of resources to identify opportunities for product development are called proactive strategies.
Proactive	To be proactive is to act before a situation becomes a source of confrontation or crisis. It is the opposite of "retroactive," which refers to actions taken after an event.
Hierarchy	A system of grouping people in an organization according to rank from the top down in which all subordinate managers must report to one person is called a hierarchy.
Trust	Trust refers to a legal relationship in which a person who has legal title to property has the duty to hold it for the use or benefit of another person. The term is also used in a general sense to mean confidence reposed in one person by another.
Productivity	Productivity refers to the total output of goods and services in a given period of time divided by work hours.
Communication	Communication refers to the social process in which two or more parties exchange information and share meaning.
Assessment	Collecting information and providing feedback to employees about their behavior, communication style, or skills is an assessment.
Personnel	A collective term for all of the employees of an organization. Personnel is also commonly used to refer to the personnel management function or the organizational unit responsible for administering personnel programs.
Downsizing	The process of eliminating managerial and non-managerial positions are called downsizing.
Restructuring	Restructuring is the corporate management term for the act of partially dismantling and reorganizing a company for the purpose of making it more efficient and therefore more profitable.

Chapter 2. MANAGING PERSONAL STRESS

Chapter 2. MANAGING PERSONAL STRESS

Efficiency	Efficiency refers to the use of minimal resources, such as raw materials, money, and people- to produce a desired volume of output.
Remainder	A remainder in property law is a future interest created in a transferee that is capable of becoming possessory upon the natural termination of a prior estate created by the same instrument.
Tactic	A short-term immediate decision that, in its totality, leads to the achievement of strategic goals is called a tactic.
Preparation	Preparation refers to usually the first stage in the creative process. It includes education and formal training.
Preventive maintenance	Maintaining scheduled upkeep and improvement to equipment so equipment can actually improve with age is called the preventive maintenance.
Continuous improvement	Constantly improving the way the organization does things so that customer needs can be better satisfied is referred to as continuous improvement.
Competency	Competency refers to a person's ability to understand the nature of the transaction and the consequences of entering into it at the time the contract was entered into.
Termination	The ending of a corporation that occurs only after the winding-up of the corporation's affairs, the liquidation of its assets, and the distribution of the proceeds to the claimants are referred to as a termination.
Stock	In financial terminology, stock is the capital raized by a corporation, through the issuance and sale of shares. A shareholder is any person or organization which owns one or more shares of a corporation's stock. The aggregate value of a corporation's issued shares is its market capitalization.
Controlling	A management function that involves determining whether or not an organization is progressing toward its goals and objectives, and taking corrective action if it is not is called controlling.
Standing	Standing refers to the legal requirement that anyone seeking to challenge a particular action in court must demonstrate that such action substantially affects his legitimate interests before he will be entitled to bring suit.
Accountability	The extent to which one must answer to higher authority-legal or organizational-for one's actions in society at large or within one's particular organizational position is an accountability.
Laggards	Laggards refer to the 16 percent of the market who have fear of debt, use friends for information sources, and accept ideas and products only after they have been long established in the market.
Delegation	Delegation is the handing of a task over to another person, usually a subordinate. It is the assignment of authority and responsibility to another person to carry out specific activities.
Acceptance	The actual or implied receipt and retention of that which is tendered or offered is the acceptance.
Competition	In business, competition occurs when rival organizations with similar products and services attempt to gain customers.
Bond	A long-term debt security that is secured by collateral is called a bond.
Loyalty	Marketers tend to define customer loyalty as making repeat purchases. Some argue that it should be defined attitudinally as a strongly positive feeling about the brand.

Chapter 2. MANAGING PERSONAL STRESS

Chapter 2. MANAGING PERSONAL STRESS

United Nations	An international organization created by multilateral treaty in 1945 to promote social and economic cooperation among nations and to protect human rights is the United Nations.
Emotional intelligence	The ability to understand one's own emotions and the emotions of people with whom one interacts on a daily basis is referred to as the emotional intelligence.
Empathy	Empathy refers to dimension of service quality-caring individualized attention provided to customers.
Confirmed	When the seller's bank agrees to assume liability on the letter of credit issued by the buyer's bank the transaction is confirmed. The term means that the credit is not only backed up by the issuing foreign bank, but that payment is also guaranteed by the notifying American bank.
Interest	Interest refers to the payment the issuer of the bond makes to the bondholders for use of the borrowed money. It is the return to capital achieved over time or as the result of an event.
Participation	Participation refers to the process of giving employees a voice in making decisions about their own work.
Authority	Authority in agency law, refers to an agent's ability to affect his principal's legal relations with third parties. Also used to refer to an actor's legal power or ability to do something. In addition, sometimes used to refer to a statute, case, or other legal source that justifies a particular result.
Task performance	The quantity and quality of work produced is referred to as the task performance. Actions taken to ensure that the work group reaches its goals.
Production	The creation of finished goods and services using the factors of production: land, labor, capital, entrepreneurship, and knowledge.
Quality control	The measurement of products and services against set standards is referred to as quality control.
Quality assurance	Those activities associated with assuring the quality of a product or service is called quality assurance.
Administration	Administration refers to the management and direction of the affairs of governments and institutions; a collective term for all policymaking officials of a government; the execution and implementation of public policy.
Social security	The term used to describe the Old-Age, Survivors, and Disability Insurance Program established by the Social Security Act of 1935 is social security.
Insurance	A means for persons and businesses to protect themselves against the risk of loss is insurance.
Work redesign	The altering of jobs to increase both the quality of employees' work experience and their productivity is referred to as work redesign.
Action steps	The part of a written affirmative plan that specifies what an employer plans to do to reduce underutilization of protected groups is referred to as action steps.
Management by objectives	Management by objectives is a process of agreeing upon objectives within an organization so that management and employees buy in to the objectives and understand what they are.
Performance appraisal	An evaluation in which the performance level of employees is measured against established standards to make decisions about promotions, compenzation, additional training, or firing is referred to as performance appraisal.
Support network	A group of two or more trainees who agree to meet and discuss their progress in using learned capabilities on the job is referred to as support network.

Go to **Cram101.com** for the Practice Tests for this Chapter.

Chapter 2. MANAGING PERSONAL STRESS

Chapter 2. MANAGING PERSONAL STRESS

Expense	An expense refers to costs involved in operating a business, such as rent, utilities, and salaries.
Evaluation	The consumer's appraisal of the product or brand on important attributes is called evaluation.
Strike	A strike is a nonviolent work stoppage for the purpose of obtaining better terms and conditions of employment under a collective bargaining agreement.
Communism	An economic and political system in which the state makes all economic decisions and owns all the major forms of production is communism.
Capitalism	An economic system in which all or most of the factors of production and distribution are privately owned and operated for profit is called capitalism.
Committee	A long-lasting, sometimes permanent team in the organization structure created to deal with tasks that recur regularly is the committee.
Promotion	Promotion refers to all the techniques sellers use to motivate people to buy products or services. An attempt by marketers to inform people about products and to persuade them to participate in an exchange.
Exhibit	Exhibit refers to a copy of a written instrument on which a pleading is founded, annexed to the pleading and by reference made a part of it. Any paper or thing offered in evidence and marked for identification.
Acquisition	A company's purchase of the property and obligations of another company is an acquisition.
Compliance	A type of influence process where a receiver accepts the position advocated by a source to obtain favorable outcomes or to avoid punishment is the compliance.
Incentive	A reward offered by a marketer to a prospective customer in return for furnishing information or making a purchase is referred to as an incentive.
Users	Users refer to people in the organization who actually use the product or service purchased by the buying center.
Testimony	In some contexts, the word bears the same import as the word evidence, but in most connections it has a much narrower meaning. Testimony are the words heard from the witness in court, and evidence is what the jury considers it worth.
Mentor	An experienced employee who supervises, coaches, and guides lower-level employees by introducing them to the right people and generally being their organizational sponsor is a mentor.
Mentoring	Mentoring refers to a developmental relationship between a more experienced mentor and a less experienced partner referred to as a mentee or protégé. Usually - but not necessarily - the mentor/protégé pair will be of the same sex.
Malcolm Baldrige National Quality Award	Malcolm Baldrige national quality award refers to U.S. national quality award sponsored by the U.S. Department of Commerce and private industry. The program aims to reward quality in the business sector, health care, and education, and was inspired by the ideas of Total Quality Management.
Teamwork	That which occurs when group members work together in ways that utilize their skills well to accomplish a purpose is called teamwork.
Holding	The holding is a court's determination of a matter of law based on the issue presented in the particular case. In other words: under this law, with these facts, this result.

Go to **Cram101.com** for the Practice Tests for this Chapter.

Chapter 2. MANAGING PERSONAL STRESS

Chapter 3. SOLVING PROBLEMS ANALYTICALLY AND CREATIVELY

Manager	A person who is formally responsible for supporting the work efforts of other people is a manager.
Brief	Brief refers to a statement of a party's case or legal arguments, usually prepared by an attorney. Also used to make legal arguments before appellate courts.
Innovation	The process of creating and doing new things that are introduced into the marketplace as products, processes, or services is innovation.
Abandonment	Abandonment in law, the relinquishment of an interest, claim, privilege or possession. This broad meaning has a number of applications in different branches of law.
Participation	Participation refers to the process of giving employees a voice in making decisions about their own work.
Evaluation	The consumer's appraisal of the product or brand on important attributes is called evaluation.
Acceptance	The actual or implied receipt and retention of that which is tendered or offered is the acceptance.
Organizational goals	Objectives that management seeks to achieve in pursuing the firm's purpose are organizational goals.
Consideration	Consideration in contract law, a basic requirement for an enforceable agreement under traditional contract principles, defined in this text as legal value, bargained for and given in exchange for an act or promise. In corporation law, cash or property contributed to a corporation in exchange for shares, or a promise to contribute such cash or property.
Budget	A financial plan that sets forth management's expectations for revenues and, based on those expectations, allocates the use of specific resources throughout the firm is called budget.
Exchange	The trade of things of value between buyer and seller so that each is better off after the trade is called the exchange.
Downsizing	The process of eliminating managerial and non-managerial positions are called downsizing.
Productivity	Productivity refers to the total output of goods and services in a given period of time divided by work hours.
Resistance to change	Resistance to change refers to an attitude or behavior that shows unwillingness to make or support a change.
Composition	An out-of-court settlement in which creditors agree to accept a fractional settlement on their original claim is referred to as composition.
Idea generation	Developing a pool of concepts as candidates for new products is called idea generation.
Efficiency	Efficiency refers to the use of minimal resources, such as raw materials, money, and people- to produce a desired volume of output.
Property	Property refers to something that is capable of being owned. A right or interest associated with something that gives the owner the ability to exercise dominion over it.
Administration	Administration refers to the management and direction of the affairs of governments and institutions; a collective term for all policymaking officials of a government; the execution and implementation of public policy.
Holding	The holding is a court's determination of a matter of law based on the issue presented in the particular case. In other words: under this law, with these facts, this result.
Production	The creation of finished goods and services using the factors of production: land, labor, capital, entrepreneurship, and knowledge.

Chapter 3. SOLVING PROBLEMS ANALYTICALLY AND CREATIVELY

Chapter 3. SOLVING PROBLEMS ANALYTICALLY AND CREATIVELY

Product	Any physical good, service, or idea that satisfies a want or need is called product. Product in project management is a physical entity created as a result of project work.
Assignment	A transfer of property or some right or interest is referred to as assignment.
Interest	Interest refers to the payment the issuer of the bond makes to the bondholders for use of the borrowed money. It is the return to capital achieved over time or as the result of an event.
Bond	A long-term debt security that is secured by collateral is called a bond.
Task force	A temporary team or committee formed to solve a specific short-term problem involving several departments is the task force.
Context	The effect of the background under which a message often takes on more and richer meaning is a context. Context is especially important in cross-cultural interactions because some cultures are said to be high context or low context.
Continuity	A media scheduling strategy where a continuous pattern of advertising is used over the time span of the advertising campaign is continuity.
Strike	A strike is a nonviolent work stoppage for the purpose of obtaining better terms and conditions of employment under a collective bargaining agreement.
Devise	In a will, a gift of real property is called a devise.
Hearing	A hearing is a proceeding before a court or other decision-making body or officer. A hearing is generally distinguished from a trial in that it is usually shorter and often less formal.
Industry	Industry refers to a group of firms offering products that are close substitutes for each other.
Sensation	Sensation refers to the immediate and direct response of the senses to a stimulus such as an advertisement, package, brand name, or point-of-purchase display.
Petition	A petition is a request to an authority, most commonly a government official or public entity. In the colloquial sense, a petition is a document addressed to some official and signed by numerous individuals.
Complexity	The technical sophistication of the product and hence the amount of understanding required to use it is referred to as complexity. It is the opposite of simplicity.
Contribution	In business organization law, the cash or property contributed to a business by its owners is referred to as contribution.
Configuration	An organization's shape, which reflects the division of labor and the means of coordinating the divided tasks is configuration.
Utility	An economic term that refers to the value or want-satisfying ability that's added to goods or services by organizations when the products are made more useful or accessible to consumers than before is a utility.
Preparation	Preparation refers to usually the first stage in the creative process. It includes education and formal training.
Verification	Verification refers to the final stage of the creative process where the validity or truthfulness of the insight is determined. The feedback portion of communication in which the receiver sends a message to the source indicating receipt of the message and the degree to which he or she understood the message.
Options	Options give the owner the right but not the obligation to buy or sell an underlying security at a set price for a given time period.
Organizational	The study of human behavior in organizational settings, the interface between human behavior

Go to **Cram101.com** for the Practice Tests for this Chapter.

Chapter 3. SOLVING PROBLEMS ANALYTICALLY AND CREATIVELY

Chapter 3. SOLVING PROBLEMS ANALYTICALLY AND CREATIVELY

Behavior	and the organization, and the organization itself is called organizational behavior.
Open system	A system that interacts with its environment is referred to as open system. It is a system that takes in (raw materials, capital, skilled labor) and converts them into goods and services (via machinery, human skills) that are sent back to that environment, where they are bought by customers.
Insurance	A means for persons and businesses to protect themselves against the risk of loss is insurance.
Policy	Similar to a script in that a policy can be a less than completely rational decision-making method. Involves the use of a pre-existing set of decision steps for any problem that presents itself.
Liability insurance	Liability insurance is designed to offer specific protection against third party claims, i.e., payment is not typically made to the insured, but rather to someone suffering loss who is not a party to the insurance contract.
Liability	A liability is anything that is a hindrance, or puts individuals at a disadvantage.
Brainstorming	Brainstorming refers to a technique designed to overcome our natural tendency to evaluate and criticize ideas and thereby reduce the creative output of those ideas. People are encouraged to produce ideas/options without criticizing, often at a very fast pace to minimize our natural tendency to criticize.
Holder	A person in possession of a document of title or an instrument payable or indorsed to him, his order, or to bearer is a holder.
Loyalty	Marketers tend to define customer loyalty as making repeat purchases. Some argue that it should be defined attitudinally as a strongly positive feeling about the brand.
Status quo	The existing state of things is the status quo. In contract law, returning a party to status quo or status quo ante means putting him in the position he was in before entering the contract.
Confirmed	When the seller's bank agrees to assume liability on the letter of credit issued by the buyer's bank the transaction is confirmed. The term means that the credit is not only backed up by the issuing foreign bank, but that payment is also guaranteed by the notifying American bank.
Management	Management characterizes the process of leading and directing all or part of an organization, often a business, through the deployment and manipulation of resources. Early twentieth-century management writer Mary Parker Follett defined management as "the art of getting things done through people."
Contract	A contract is a "promise" or an "agreement" that is enforced or recognized by the law. In the civil law, contracts are considered to be part of the general law of obligations. This article describes the law relating to contracts in common law jurisdictions.
Forming	The first stage of team development, where the team is formed and the objectives for the team are set is referred to as forming.
Devil's advocate	A decision-making technique in which an individual is assigned the role of challenging the assumptions and assertions made by the group to prevent premature consensus is the devil's advocate.
Groupthink	Groupthink is a situation in which pressures for cohesion and togetherness are so strong as to produce narrowly considered and bad decisions; this can be especially true via conformity pressures in groups.
Competition	In business, competition occurs when rival organizations with similar products and services

Go to Cram101.com for the Practice Tests for this Chapter.

Chapter 3. SOLVING PROBLEMS ANALYTICALLY AND CREATIVELY

Chapter 3. SOLVING PROBLEMS ANALYTICALLY AND CREATIVELY

	attempt to gain customers.
Accountability	The extent to which one must answer to higher authority-legal or organizational-for one's actions in society at large or within one's particular organizational position is an accountability.
Economy	The income, expenditures, and resources that affect the cost of running a business and household are called an economy.
Trade show	A type of exhibition or forum where manufacturers can display their products to current as well as prospective buyers is referred to as trade show.
Corporation	A form of business organization that is owned by owners, called shareholders, who have no inherent right to manage the business, and is managed by a board of directors that is elected by the shareholders is called a corporation.
Communication	Communication refers to the social process in which two or more parties exchange information and share meaning.
Competitor	Other organizations in the same industry or type of business that provide a good or service to the same set of customers is referred to as a competitor.
Users	Users refer to people in the organization who actually use the product or service purchased by the buying center.
Complaint	The pleading in a civil case in which the plaintiff states his claim and requests relief is called complaint. In the common law, it is a formal legal document that sets out the basic facts and legal reasons that the filing party (the plaintiffs) believes are sufficient to support a claim against another person, persons, entity or entities (the defendants) that entitles the plaintiff(s) to a remedy (either money damages or injunctive relief).
Idea champion	A person who sees the need for and promotes productive change within the organization is referred to as an idea champion.
Facilitator	A facilitator is someone who skilfully helps a group of people understand their common objectives and plan to achieve them without personally taking any side of the argument.
Mentor	An experienced employee who supervises, coaches, and guides lower-level employees by introducing them to the right people and generally being their organizational sponsor is a mentor.
Pawn	In law a pledge (also pawn) is a bailment of personal property as a security for some debt or engagement
Marketing	The American Marketing Association suggests that Marketing is "the process of planning and executing the pricing, promotion, and distribution of goods, ideas, and services to create exchanges that satisfy individual and organizational goals."
Bid	Bid refers to make an offer at an auction or at a judicial sale.

Go to Cram101.com for the Practice Tests for this Chapter.

Chapter 3. SOLVING PROBLEMS ANALYTICALLY AND CREATIVELY

Chapter 4. COACHING, COUNSELING, AND SUPPORTIVE COMMUNICATION

Communication	Communication refers to the social process in which two or more parties exchange information and share meaning.
Management	Management characterizes the process of leading and directing all or part of an organization, often a business, through the deployment and manipulation of resources. Early twentieth-century management writer Mary Parker Follett defined management as "the art of getting things done through people."
Context	The effect of the background under which a message often takes on more and richer meaning is a context. Context is especially important in cross-cultural interactions because some cultures are said to be high context or low context.
Trust	Trust refers to a legal relationship in which a person who has legal title to property has the duty to hold it for the use or benefit of another person. The term is also used in a general sense to mean confidence reposed in one person by another.
Effective communication	When the intended meaning equals the perceived meaning it is called effective communication.
Manager	A person who is formally responsible for supporting the work efforts of other people is a manager.
Comprehensive	A comprehensive refers to a layout accurate in size, color, scheme, and other necessary details to show how a final ad will look. For presentation only, never for reproduction.
Organizational communication	Thee process by which information is exchanged n the organizational setting is organizational communication.
Product	Any physical good, service, or idea that satisfies a want or need is called product. Product in project management is a physical entity created as a result of project work.
Consideration	Consideration in contract law, a basic requirement for an enforceable agreement under traditional contract principles, defined in this text as legal value, bargained for and given in exchange for an act or promise. In corporation law, cash or property contributed to a corporation in exchange for shares, or a promise to contribute such cash or property.
Receiver	A person that is appointed as a custodian of other people's property by a court of law or a creditor of the owner, pending a lawsuit or reorganization is called a receiver.
Information technology	Information technology refers to technology that helps companies change business by allowing them to use new methods.
Competitive advantage	A business is said to have a competitive advantage when its unique strengths, often based on cost, quality, time, and innovation, offer consumers a greater percieved value and there by differtiating it from its competitors.
Productivity	Productivity refers to the total output of goods and services in a given period of time divided by work hours.
Acceptance	The actual or implied receipt and retention of that which is tendered or offered is the acceptance.
Competency	Competency refers to a person's ability to understand the nature of the transaction and the consequences of entering into it at the time the contract was entered into.
Competitor	Other organizations in the same industry or type of business that provide a good or service to the same set of customers is referred to as a competitor.
Capital	Contributions of money and other property to a business made by the owners of the business are capital.
Delegation	Delegation is the handing of a task over to another person, usually a subordinate. It is the

Go to **Cram101.com** for the Practice Tests for this Chapter.

Chapter 4. COACHING, COUNSELING, AND SUPPORTIVE COMMUNICATION

Chapter 4. COACHING, COUNSELING, AND SUPPORTIVE COMMUNICATION

	assignment of authority and responsibility to another person to carry out specific activities.
Authority	Authority in agency law, refers to an agent's ability to affect his principal's legal relations with third parties. Also used to refer to an actor's legal power or ability to do something. In addition, sometimes used to refer to a statute, case, or other legal source that justifies a particular result.
Resistance to change	Resistance to change refers to an attitude or behavior that shows unwillingness to make or support a change.
Strike	A strike is a nonviolent work stoppage for the purpose of obtaining better terms and conditions of employment under a collective bargaining agreement.
Content	Content refers to all digital information included on a website, including the presentation form-text, video, audio, and graphics.
Evaluation	The consumer's appraisal of the product or brand on important attributes is called evaluation.
Confirmed	When the seller's bank agrees to assume liability on the letter of credit issued by the buyer's bank the transaction is confirmed. The term means that the credit is not only backed up by the issuing foreign bank, but that payment is also guaranteed by the notifying American bank.
Standing	Standing refers to the legal requirement that anyone seeking to challenge a particular action in court must demonstrate that such action substantially affects his legitimate interests before he will be entitled to bring suit.
Committee	A long-lasting, sometimes permanent team in the organization structure created to deal with tasks that recur regularly is the committee.
Jargon	Jargon is terminology, much like slang, that relates to a specific activity, profession, or group. It develops as a kind of shorthand, to express ideas that are frequently discussed between members of a group, and can also have the effect of distinguishing those belonging to a group from those who are not.
Contribution	In business organization law, the cash or property contributed to a business by its owners is referred to as contribution.
Collaboration	Collaboration occurs when the interaction between groups is very important to goal attainment and the goals are compatible. Wherein people work together —applying both to the work of individuals as well as larger collectives and societies.
Teamwork	That which occurs when group members work together in ways that utilize their skills well to accomplish a purpose is called teamwork.
Standard of living	The amount of goods and services people can buy with the money they have is called standard of living.
Controlling	A management function that involves determining whether or not an organization is progressing toward its goals and objectives, and taking corrective action if it is not is called controlling.
Variance	In budgeting a variance is a difference between budgeted, planned or standard amount and the actual amount incurred/sold.
Personnel	A collective term for all of the employees of an organization. Personnel is also commonly used to refer to the personnel management function or the organizational unit responsible for administering personnel programs.

Go to **Cram101.com** for the Practice Tests for this Chapter.

Chapter 4. COACHING, COUNSELING, AND SUPPORTIVE COMMUNICATION

Chapter 4. COACHING, COUNSELING, AND SUPPORTIVE COMMUNICATION

Empathy	Empathy refers to dimension of service quality-caring individualized attention provided to customers.
Hearing	A hearing is a proceeding before a court or other decision-making body or officer. A hearing is generally distinguished from a trial in that it is usually shorter and often less formal.
Exchange	The trade of things of value between buyer and seller so that each is better off after the trade is called the exchange.
Complaint	The pleading in a civil case in which the plaintiff states his claim and requests relief is called complaint. In the common law, it is a formal legal document that sets out the basic facts and legal reasons that the filing party (the plaintiffs) believes are sufficient to support a claim against another person, persons, entity or entities (the defendants) that entitles the plaintiff(s) to a remedy (either money damages or injunctive relief).
Holding	The holding is a court's determination of a matter of law based on the issue presented in the particular case. In other words: under this law, with these facts, this result.
Bond	A long-term debt security that is secured by collateral is called a bond.
Negotiation	Negotiation is the process whereby interested parties resolve disputes, agree upon courses of action, bargain for individual or collective advantage, and/or attempt to craft outcomes which serve their mutual interests.
Policy	Similar to a script in that a policy can be a less than completely rational decision-making method. Involves the use of a pre-existing set of decision steps for any problem that presents itself.
Contract	A contract is a "promise" or an "agreement" that is enforced or recognized by the law. In the civil law, contracts are considered to be part of the general law of obligations. This article describes the law relating to contracts in common law jurisdictions.
Informal contract	Informal contract refers to a contract where the parties have not attempted to spell out all the terms. A valid informal contract is fully enforceable and may be sued upon if breached.
Mistake	In contract law a mistake is incorrect understanding by one or more parties to a contract and may be used as grounds to invalidate the agreement. Common law has identified three different types of mistake in contract: unilateral mistake, mutual mistake, and common mistake.
Accountability	The extent to which one must answer to higher authority-legal or organizational-for one's actions in society at large or within one's particular organizational position is an accountability.
Continuous improvement	Constantly improving the way the organization does things so that customer needs can be better satisfied is referred to as continuous improvement.
Efficiency	Efficiency refers to the use of minimal resources, such as raw materials, money, and people-to produce a desired volume of output.
Emotional intelligence	The ability to understand one's own emotions and the emotions of people with whom one interacts on a daily basis is referred to as the emotional intelligence.
Effective manager	Leader of a team that consistently achieves high performance goals is an effective manager.

Chapter 4. COACHING, COUNSELING, AND SUPPORTIVE COMMUNICATION

Chapter 5. GAINING POWER AND INFLUENCE

Manager	A person who is formally responsible for supporting the work efforts of other people is a manager.
Management	Management characterizes the process of leading and directing all or part of an organization, often a business, through the deployment and manipulation of resources. Early twentieth-century management writer Mary Parker Follett defined management as "the art of getting things done through people."
Assessment	Collecting information and providing feedback to employees about their behavior, communication style, or skills is an assessment.
Shareholder	Shareholder refers to an owner of a corporation, who has no inherent right to manage the corporation but has liability limited to his capital contribution.
Unions	Employee organizations that have the main goal of representing members in employeemanagement bargaining over job-related issues are called unions.
Union	A union refers to employee organizations that have the main goal of representing members in employeemanagement bargaining over job-related issues.
Product	Any physical good, service, or idea that satisfies a want or need is called product. Product in project management is a physical entity created as a result of project work.
Authority	Authority in agency law, refers to an agent's ability to affect his principal's legal relations with third parties. Also used to refer to an actor's legal power or ability to do something. In addition, sometimes used to refer to a statute, case, or other legal source that justifies a particular result.
Argument	The discussion by counsel for the respective parties of their contentions on the law and the facts of the case being tried in order to aid the jury in arriving at a correct and just conclusion is called argument.
Public relations	Public relations refers to the management function that evaluates public attitudes, changes policies and procedures in response to the public's requests, and executes a program of action and information to earn public understanding and acceptance.
Budget	A financial plan that sets forth management's expectations for revenues and, based on those expectations, allocates the use of specific resources throughout the firm is called budget.
Promotion	Promotion refers to all the techniques sellers use to motivate people to buy products or services. An attempt by marketers to inform people about products and to persuade them to participate in an exchange.
Dictum	Dictum refers to language in a judicial opinion that is not necessary for the decision of the case and that, while perhaps persuasive, does not bind subsequent courts.
Preparation	Preparation refers to usually the first stage in the creative process. It includes education and formal training.
Empowerment	Giving employees the authority and responsibility to respond quickly to customer requests is called empowerment.
Warrant	A warrant is a security that entitles the holder to buy or sell a certain additional quantity of an underlying security at an agreed-upon price, at the holder's discretion.
Yield	The interest rate that equates a future value or an annuity to a given present value is a yield.
Hierarchy	A system of grouping people in an organization according to rank from the top down in which all subordinate managers must report to one person is called a hierarchy.
Virtual	A temporary alliance between two or more organizations that band together to undertake a

Go to **Cram101.com** for the Practice Tests for this Chapter.

Chapter 5. GAINING POWER AND INFLUENCE

Chapter 5. GAINING POWER AND INFLUENCE

organization	specific venture is a virtual organization.
Structural change	Any change in the way in which an organization is designed and managed is referred to as a structural change.
Small business	Small business refers to a business that is independently owned and operated, is not dominant in its field of operation, and meets certain standards of size in terms of employees or annual receipts.
Contribution	In business organization law, the cash or property contributed to a business by its owners is referred to as contribution.
Mentor	An experienced employee who supervises, coaches, and guides lower-level employees by introducing them to the right people and generally being their organizational sponsor is a mentor.
Context	The effect of the background under which a message often takes on more and richer meaning is a context. Context is especially important in cross-cultural interactions because some cultures are said to be high context or low context.
Civil service	A collective term for all nonmilitary employees of a government. Paramilitary organizations, such as police and firefighters, are always included in civil service counts in the United States. Civil service employment is not the same as merit system employment, because all patronage positions are included in civil service totals.
Position power	Position power refers to power manager's hold due to their role in the organization. May include a manager's network of contacts, legitimate authority and control over information, rewards, punishments, and the work environment.
Capital	Contributions of money and other property to a business made by the owners of the business are capital.
Human capital	The economic value of the knowledge, experience, skills, and capabilities of employees is called human capital.
Competencies	An organization's special capabilities, including skills, technologies, and resources that distinguish it from other organizations are competencies.
Leverage	Leverage is using given resources in such a way that the potential positive or negative outcome is magnified. In finance, this generally refers to borrowing.
Appeal	Appeal refers to the act of asking an appellate court to overturn a decision after the trial court's final judgment has been entered.
Credibility	The extent to which a source is perceived as having knowledge, skill, or experience relevant to a communication topic and can be trusted to give an unbiased opinion or present objective information on the issue is called credibility.
Commerce	Commerce is the exchange of something of value between two entities. It is the central mechanism from which capitalism is derived.
E-commerce	The sale of goods and services by computer over the Internet is referred to as the e-commerce.
Self-directed learning	A program in which employees take responsibility for all aspects of learning is referred to as self-directed learning.
Evaluation	The consumer's appraisal of the product or brand on important attributes is called evaluation.
Preponderance	Preponderance of the evidence means that evidence, in the judgment of the juror, is entitled to the greatest weight, appears to be more credible, has greater force, and overcomes not

Chapter 5. GAINING POWER AND INFLUENCE

Chapter 5. GAINING POWER AND INFLUENCE

	only the opposing presumptions, but also the opposing evidence.
Preference	The act of a debtor in paying or securing one or more of his creditors in a manner more favorable to them than to other creditors or to the exclusion of such other creditors is a preference. In the absence of statute, a preference is perfectly good, but to be legal it must be bona fide, and not a mere subterfuge of the debtor to secure a future benefit to himself or to prevent the application of his property to his debts.
Trust	Trust refers to a legal relationship in which a person who has legal title to property has the duty to hold it for the use or benefit of another person. The term is also used in a general sense to mean confidence reposed in one person by another.
Accounting	The recording, classifying, summarizing, and interpreting of financial events and transactions to provide management and other interested parties the information they need to make good decisions is called accounting.
Expert power	The extent to which a person controls information that is valuable to someone else is referred to as expert power.
Attractiveness	A source characteristic that makes him or her appealing to a message recipient is attractiveness. Source attractiveness can be based on similarity, familiarity, or likeability.
Charisma	A form of interpersonal attraction that inspires support and acceptance from others is charisma. It refers especially to a quality in certain people who easily draw the attention and admiration (or even hatred if the charisma is negative) of others due to a "magnetic" quality of personality and/or appearance.
Charismatic leader	A leader who has the ability to motivate subordinates to transcend their expected performance is a charismatic leader.
Mistake	In contract law a mistake is incorrect understanding by one or more parties to a contract and may be used as grounds to invalidate the agreement. Common law has identified three different types of mistake in contract: unilateral mistake, mutual mistake, and common mistake.
Advertising	Advertising refers to paid, nonpersonal communication through various media by organizations and individuals who are in some way identified in the advertising message.
Best efforts	Best efforts refer to a distribution in which the investment banker agrees to work for a commission rather than actually underwriting the issue for resale. It is a procedure that is used by smaller investment bankers with relatively unknown companies. The investment banker is not directly taking the risk for distribution.
Human resources	Human resources refers to the individuals within the firm, and to the portion of the firm's organization that deals with hiring, firing, training, and other personnel issues.
Distribution	Distribution is one of the four aspects of marketing. A distribution business is the middleman between the manufacturer and retailer or (usually)in commercial or industrial the business customer.
Production	The creation of finished goods and services using the factors of production: land, labor, capital, entrepreneurship, and knowledge.
Cognitive dissonance	The anxiety a person experiences when he or she simultaneously possesses two sets of knowledge or perceptions that are contradictory or incongruent is referred to as the cognitive dissonance.
Policy	Similar to a script in that a policy can be a less than completely rational decision-making method. Involves the use of a pre-existing set of decision steps for any problem that presents itself.

Go to **Cram101.com** for the Practice Tests for this Chapter.

Chapter 5. GAINING POWER AND INFLUENCE

Chapter 5. GAINING POWER AND INFLUENCE

Targeting	Targeting refers to the ability to address personalized promotions to a particular person who may be identified or described by means of an anonymous profile.
Value system	A value system refers to how an individual or a group of individuals organize their ethical or ideological values. A well-defined value system is a moral code.
Acceptance	The actual or implied receipt and retention of that which is tendered or offered is the acceptance.
Economy	The income, expenditures, and resources that affect the cost of running a business and household are called an economy.
Loyalty	Marketers tend to define customer loyalty as making repeat purchases. Some argue that it should be defined attitudinally as a strongly positive feeling about the brand.
Premium	Premium refers to the fee charged by an insurance company for an insurance policy. The rate of losses must be relatively predictable: In order to set the premium (prices) insurers must be able to estimate them accurately.
Marketing	The American Marketing Association suggests that Marketing is "the process of planning and executing the pricing, promotion, and distribution of goods, ideas, and services to create exchanges that satisfy individual and organizational goals."
Insurance	A means for persons and businesses to protect themselves against the risk of loss is insurance.
Edict	Edict refers to a command or prohibition promulgated by a sovereign and having the effect of
Personnel	A collective term for all of the employees of an organization. Personnel is also commonly used to refer to the personnel management function or the organizational unit responsible for administering personnel programs.
Organizational commitment	A person's identification with and attachment to an organization is called organizational commitment.
Corporation	A form of business organization that is owned by owners, called shareholders, who have no inherent right to manage the business, and is managed by a board of directors that is elected by the shareholders is called a corporation.
Efficiency	Efficiency refers to the use of minimal resources, such as raw materials, money, and people- to produce a desired volume of output.
Communication	Communication refers to the social process in which two or more parties exchange information and share meaning.
Organizational culture	Widely shared values within an organization that provide coherence and cooperation to achieve common goals are referred to as a organizational culture.
Cultural values	The values that employees need to have and act on for the organization to act on the strategic values are called cultural values.
Asset	In business and accounting an asset is anything owned which can produce future economic benefit, whether in possession or by right to take possession, by a person or a group acting together, e.g. a company, the measurement of which can be expressed in monetary terms. Asset is listed on the balance sheet. It has a normal balance of debit.
Visibility	Visibility is used in marketing, as a measure of how much the public sees a product or its advertising.
Forming	The first stage of team development, where the team is formed and the objectives for the team are set is referred to as forming.

Go to **Cram101.com** for the Practice Tests for this Chapter.

Chapter 5. GAINING POWER AND INFLUENCE

Chapter 5. GAINING POWER AND INFLUENCE

Innovation	The process of creating and doing new things that are introduced into the marketplace as products, processes, or services is innovation.
Participation	Participation refers to the process of giving employees a voice in making decisions about their own work.
Conglomerate	Conglomerate refers to a corporation that is made up of many diverse, often unrelated divisions. This form of organization is thought to reduce risk, but may create problems of coordination.
Committee	A long-lasting, sometimes permanent team in the organization structure created to deal with tasks that recur regularly is the committee.
Task force	A temporary team or committee formed to solve a specific short-term problem involving several departments is the task force.
Industry	Industry refers to a group of firms offering products that are close substitutes for each other.
Closing	The finalization of a real estate sales transaction that passes title to the property from the seller to the buyer is referred to as a closing. Closing is a sales term which refers to the process of making a sale. It refers to reaching the final step, which may be an exchange of money or acquiring a signature.
Merger	Merger in corporation law, traditionally refers to a transaction by which one corporation acquires another corporation, with the acquiring corporation being owned by the shareholders of both corporations and the acquired corporation going out of existence. Today, loosely applied to any negotiated acquisition of one corporation by another.
Utility	An economic term that refers to the value or want-satisfying ability that's added to goods or services by organizations when the products are made more useful or accessible to consumers than before is a utility.
Interest	Interest refers to the payment the issuer of the bond makes to the bondholders for use of the borrowed money. It is the return to capital achieved over time or as the result of an event.
Holder	A person in possession of a document of title or an instrument payable or indorsed to him, his order, or to bearer is a holder.
Compliance	A type of influence process where a receiver accepts the position advocated by a source to obtain favorable outcomes or to avoid punishment is the compliance.
Reciprocity	An industrial buying practice in which two organizations agree to purchase each other's products and services is called reciprocity.
Strike	A strike is a nonviolent work stoppage for the purpose of obtaining better terms and conditions of employment under a collective bargaining agreement.
Exchange	The trade of things of value between buyer and seller so that each is better off after the trade is called the exchange.
Interdependence	The extent to which departments depend on each other for resources or materials to accomplish their tasks is referred to as interdependence.
Tactic	A short-term immediate decision that, in its totality, leads to the achievement of strategic goals is called a tactic.
Alienation	The voluntary act or acts by which one-person transfers his or her own property to another is referred to as alienation.
Incentive	A reward offered by a marketer to a prospective customer in return for furnishing information or making a purchase is referred to as an incentive.

Chapter 5. GAINING POWER AND INFLUENCE

Chapter 5. GAINING POWER AND INFLUENCE

Assignment	A transfer of property or some right or interest is referred to as assignment.
Negotiation	Negotiation is the process whereby interested parties resolve disputes, agree upon courses of action, bargain for individual or collective advantage, and/or attempt to craft outcomes which serve their mutual interests.
Organizational goals	Objectives that management seeks to achieve in pursuing the firm's purpose are organizational goals.
Accountability	The extent to which one must answer to higher authority-legal or organizational-for one's actions in society at large or within one's particular organizational position is an accountability.
Principal	In agency law, one under whose direction an agent acts and for whose benefit that agent acts is a principal.
Consequential	Damages that do not flow directly and immediately from an act but rather flow from the results of the act are consequential.
Complaint	The pleading in a civil case in which the plaintiff states his claim and requests relief is called complaint. In the common law, it is a formal legal document that sets out the basic facts and legal reasons that the filing party (the plaintiffs) believes are sufficient to support a claim against another person, persons, entity or entities (the defendants) that entitles the plaintiff(s) to a remedy (either money damages or injunctive relief).
Brief	Brief refers to a statement of a party's case or legal arguments, usually prepared by an attorney. Also used to make legal arguments before appellate courts.
Compromise	Compromise occurs when the interaction is moderately important to meeting goals and the goals are neither completely compatible nor completely incompatible.
Content	Content refers to all digital information included on a website, including the presentation form-text, video, audio, and graphics.
Bail	Bail refers to an amount of money the defendant pays to the court upon release from custody as security that he or she will return for trial.
Negligence	The omission to do something that a reasonable person, guided by those considerations that ordinarily regulate human affairs, would do, or doing something that a prudent and reasonable person would not do is negligence.

Chapter 5. GAINING POWER AND INFLUENCE

Chapter 6. MOTIVATING OTHERS

Economy	The income, expenditures, and resources that affect the cost of running a business and household are called an economy.
Bottom line	Bottom line refers to the last line in a profit and loss statement; it refers to net profit.
Annual report	Annual report refers to a yearly statement of the financial condition and progress of an organization.
Industry	Industry refers to a group of firms offering products that are close substitutes for each other.
Facilitation	Facilitation refers to helping a team or individual achieve a goal. Often used in meetings or with teams to help the teams achieve their objectives.
Manager	A person who is formally responsible for supporting the work efforts of other people is a manager.
Interest	Interest refers to the payment the issuer of the bond makes to the bondholders for use of the borrowed money. It is the return to capital achieved over time or as the result of an event.
Human resources	Human resources refers to the individuals within the firm, and to the portion of the firm's organization that deals with hiring, firing, training, and other personnel issues.
Aptitude	An aptitude is an innate inborn ability to do a certain kind of work. Aptitudes may be physical or mental. Many of them have been identified and are testable.
Product	Any physical good, service, or idea that satisfies a want or need is called product. Product in project management is a physical entity created as a result of project work.
Applicant	In many tribunal and administrative law suits, the person who initiates the claim is called the applicant.
Personnel	A collective term for all of the employees of an organization. Personnel is also commonly used to refer to the personnel management function or the organizational unit responsible for administering personnel programs.
Authority	Authority in agency law, refers to an agent's ability to affect his principal's legal relations with third parties. Also used to refer to an actor's legal power or ability to do something. In addition, sometimes used to refer to a statute, case, or other legal source that justifies a particular result.
Assessment	Collecting information and providing feedback to employees about their behavior, communication style, or skills is an assessment.
Management	Management characterizes the process of leading and directing all or part of an organization, often a business, through the deployment and manipulation of resources. Early twentieth-century management writer Mary Parker Follett defined management as "the art of getting things done through people."
Tactic	A short-term immediate decision that, in its totality, leads to the achievement of strategic goals is called a tactic.
Confirmed	When the seller's bank agrees to assume liability on the letter of credit issued by the buyer's bank the transaction is confirmed. The term means that the credit is not only backed up by the issuing foreign bank, but that payment is also guaranteed by the notifying American bank.
Compliance	A type of influence process where a receiver accepts the position advocated by a source to obtain favorable outcomes or to avoid punishment is the compliance.
Budget	A financial plan that sets forth management's expectations for revenues and, based on those expectations, allocates the use of specific resources throughout the firm is called budget.

Go to **Cram101.com** for the Practice Tests for this Chapter.

Chapter 6. MOTIVATING OTHERS

Chapter 6. MOTIVATING OTHERS

Principal	In agency law, one under whose direction an agent acts and for whose benefit that agent acts is a principal.
Options	Options give the owner the right but not the obligation to buy or sell an underlying security at a set price for a given time period.
Interpersonal skills	Interpersonal skills are used to communicate with, understand, and motivate individuals and groups.
Termination	The ending of a corporation that occurs only after the winding-up of the corporation's affairs, the liquidation of its assets, and the distribution of the proceeds to the claimants are referred to as a termination.
Production	The creation of finished goods and services using the factors of production: land, labor, capital, entrepreneurship, and knowledge.
Contribution	In business organization law, the cash or property contributed to a business by its owners is referred to as contribution.
Productivity	Productivity refers to the total output of goods and services in a given period of time divided by work hours.
Holding	The holding is a court's determination of a matter of law based on the issue presented in the particular case. In other words: under this law, with these facts, this result.
Change agent	A change agent is someone who engages either deliberately or whose behavior results in social, cultural or behavioral change. This can be studied scientifically and effective techniques can be discovered and employed.
Agent	One who acts under the direction of a principal for the principal's benefit in a legal relationship known as agency is called agent.
Accountability	The extent to which one must answer to higher authority-legal or organizational-for one's actions in society at large or within one's particular organizational position is an accountability.
Reengineering	The fundamental rethinking and radical redesign of organizational processes to achieve dramatic improvements in critical measures of performance is reengineering.
Competition	In business, competition occurs when rival organizations with similar products and services attempt to gain customers.
Trust	Trust refers to a legal relationship in which a person who has legal title to property has the duty to hold it for the use or benefit of another person. The term is also used in a general sense to mean confidence reposed in one person by another.
Consideration	Consideration in contract law, a basic requirement for an enforceable agreement under traditional contract principles, defined in this text as legal value, bargained for and given in exchange for an act or promise. In corporation law, cash or property contributed to a corporation in exchange for shares, or a promise to contribute such cash or property.
Remainder	A remainder in property law is a future interest created in a transferee that is capable of becoming possessory upon the natural termination of a prior estate created by the same instrument.
Comprehensive	A comprehensive refers to a layout accurate in size, color, scheme, and other necessary details to show how a final ad will look. For presentation only, never for reproduction.
Enabling	Enabling refers to giving workers the education and tools they need to assume their new decision-making powers.
Acceptance	The actual or implied receipt and retention of that which is tendered or offered is the

Go to Cram101.com for the Practice Tests for this Chapter.

Chapter 6. MOTIVATING OTHERS

Chapter 6. MOTIVATING OTHERS

	acceptance.
Management by objectives	Management by objectives is a process of agreeing upon objectives within an organization so that management and employees buy in to the objectives and understand what they are.
Exhibit	Exhibit refers to a copy of a written instrument on which a pleading is founded, annexed to the pleading and by reference made a part of it. Any paper or thing offered in evidence and marked for identification.
Participation	Participation refers to the process of giving employees a voice in making decisions about their own work.
Assignment	A transfer of property or some right or interest is referred to as assignment.
Content	Content refers to all digital information included on a website, including the presentation form-text, video, audio, and graphics.
Alienation	The voluntary act or acts by which one-person transfers his or her own property to another is referred to as alienation.
Management philosophy	Management philosophy refers to a philosophy that links key goal-related issues with key collaboration issues to come up with general ways by which the firm will manage its affairs.
Intervention	A proceeding by which one not originally made a party to an action or suit is permitted, on his own application, to appear therein and join one of the original parties in maintaining his cause of action or defense, or to assert some cause of action against some or all of the parties to the proceeding as originally instituted is an intervention.
Controlling	A management function that involves determining whether or not an organization is progressing toward its goals and objectives, and taking corrective action if it is not is called controlling.
Hearing	A hearing is a proceeding before a court or other decision-making body or officer. A hearing is generally distinguished from a trial in that it is usually shorter and often less formal.
Publicity	Publicity refers to any information about an individual, product, or organization that's distributed to the public through the media and that's not paid for or controlled by the seller.
Stock	In financial terminology, stock is the capital raised by a corporation, through the issuance and sale of shares. A shareholder is any person or organization which owns one or more shares of a corporation's stock. The aggregate value of a corporation's issued shares is its market capitalization.
Compensation	A payment that is given or recieved as reparation for a service or loss is referred to as compensation.
Acquisition	A company's purchase of the property and obligations of another company is an acquisition.
Competencies	An organization's special capabilities, including skills, technologies, and resources that distinguish it from other organizations are competencies.
Mentor	An experienced employee who supervises, coaches, and guides lower-level employees by introducing them to the right people and generally being their organizational sponsor is a mentor.
Organizational goals	Objectives that management seeks to achieve in pursuing the firm's purpose are organizational goals.
Skill-based pay	Pay based on the skills employees acquire and are capable of using is skill-based pay.
Collaboration	Collaboration occurs when the interaction between groups is very important to goal attainment

Go to **Cram101.com** for the Practice Tests for this Chapter.

Chapter 6. MOTIVATING OTHERS

Chapter 6. MOTIVATING OTHERS

	and the goals are compatible. Wherein people work together —applying both to the work of individuals as well as larger collectives and societies.
Cultural values	The values that employees need to have and act on for the organization to act on the strategic values are called cultural values.
Targeting	Targeting refers to the ability to address personalized promotions to a particular person who may be identified or described by means of an anonymous profile.
Promotion	Promotion refers to all the techniques sellers use to motivate people to buy products or services. An attempt by marketers to inform people about products and to persuade them to participate in an exchange.
Idea champion	A person who sees the need for and promotes productive change within the organization is referred to as an idea champion.
Task performance	The quantity and quality of work produced is referred to as the task performance. Actions taken to ensure that the work group reaches its goals.
Leverage	Leverage is using given resources in such a way that the potential positive or negative outcome is magnified. In finance, this generally refers to borrowing.
Effective manager	Leader of a team that consistently achieves high performance goals is an effective manager.
Incentive	A reward offered by a marketer to a prospective customer in return for furnishing information or making a purchase is referred to as an incentive.
Innovation	The process of creating and doing new things that are introduced into the marketplace as products, processes, or services is innovation.
Evaluation	The consumer's appraisal of the product or brand on important attributes is called evaluation.
Channel	Channel, in communications (sometimes called communications channel), refers to the medium used to convey information from a sender (or transmitter) to a receiver.
Trial	An examination before a competent tribunal, according to the law of the land, of the facts or law put in issue in a cause, for the purpose of determining such issue is a trial. When the court hears and determines any issue of fact or law for the purpose of determining the rights of the parties, it may be considered a trial.
Person-job fit	Person-job fit refers to the extent to which the contributions made by the individual match the inducements offered by the organization.
Client	The organizations with the products, services, or causes to be marketed and for which advertising agencies and other marketing promotional firms provide services is referred to as a client.
Insurance	A means for persons and businesses to protect themselves against the risk of loss is insurance.
Distribution	Distribution is one of the four aspects of marketing. A distribution business is the middleman between the manufacturer and retailer or (usually)in commercial or industrial the business customer.
Administration	Administration refers to the management and direction of the affairs of governments and institutions; a collective term for all policymaking officials of a government; the execution and implementation of public policy.
Social security	The term used to describe the Old-Age, Survivors, and Disability Insurance Program established by the Social Security Act of 1935 is social security.

Go to Cram101.com for the Practice Tests for this Chapter.

Chapter 6. MOTIVATING OTHERS

Chapter 6. MOTIVATING OTHERS

Specific performance	A contract remedy whereby the defendant is ordered to perform according to the terms of his contract is referred to as specific performance.
Accounting	The recording, classifying, summarizing, and interpreting of financial events and transactions to provide management and other interested parties the information they need to make good decisions is called accounting.
Takeover	A takeover in business refers to one company (the acquirer) purchasing another (the target). Such events resemble mergers, but without the formation of a new company.
Affiliation	A relationship with other websites in which a company can cross-promote and is credited for sales that accrue through their site is an affiliation.
Preference	The act of a debtor in paying or securing one or more of his creditors in a manner more favorable to them than to other creditors or to the exclusion of such other creditors is a preference. In the absence of statute, a preference is perfectly good, but to be legal it must be bona fide, and not a mere subterfuge of the debtor to secure a future benefit to himself or to prevent the application of his property to his debts.
Equity	Equity is the name given to the set of legal principles, in countries following the English common law tradition, which supplement strict rules of law where their application would operate harshly, so as to achieve what is sometimes referred to as "natural justice."
Advertising	Advertising refers to paid, nonpersonal communication through various media by organizations and individuals who are in some way identified in the advertising message.
Incentive system	An incentive system refers to plans in which employees can earn additional compenzation in return for certain types of performance.
Mistake	In contract law a mistake is incorrect understanding by one or more parties to a contract and may be used as grounds to invalidate the agreement. Common law has identified three different types of mistake in contract: unilateral mistake, mutual mistake, and common mistake.
Attractiveness	A source characteristic that makes him or her appealing to a message recipient is attractiveness. Source attractiveness can be based on similarity, familiarity, or likeability.
Stockbroker	A registered representative who works as a market intermediary to buy and sell securities for clients is a stockbroker.
Fringe benefits	Benefits such as sick-leave pay, vacation pay, pension plans, and health plans that represent additional compensation to employees beyond base wages are fringe benefits.
Fringe benefit	Benefits such as sick-leave pay, vacation pay, pension plans, and health plans that represent additional compenzation to employees beyond base wages is a fringe benefit.
Loyalty	Marketers tend to define customer loyalty as making repeat purchases. Some argue that it should be defined attitudinally as a strongly positive feeling about the brand.
Policy	Similar to a script in that a policy can be a less than completely rational decision-making method. Involves the use of a pre-existing set of decision steps for any problem that presents itself.
Unfairness	A concept used by the Federal Trade Commission to determine unfair or deceptive advertising practices. Unfairness occurs when a trade practice causes substantial physical or economic injury to consumers, could not be avoided by consumers, and must not be outweighed by countervailing benefits to consumers or competition.
Grant	Grant refers to an intergovernmental transfer of funds . Since the New Deal, state and local governments have become increasingly dependent upon federal grants for an almost infinite variety of programs.

Go to **Cram101.com** for the Practice Tests for this Chapter.

Chapter 6. MOTIVATING OTHERS

Chapter 6. MOTIVATING OTHERS

Stock option	A stock option is a specific type of option that uses the stock itself as an underlying instrument to determine the option's pay-off (and therefore its value). Thus it is a contract to buy (known as a "call option") or sell (known as a "put option") a certain number of shares of stock, at a predetermined or calculable (from a formula in the contract) price.
Hierarchy	A system of grouping people in an organization according to rank from the top down in which all subordinate managers must report to one person is called a hierarchy.
Brief	Brief refers to a statement of a party's case or legal arguments, usually prepared by an attorney. Also used to make legal arguments before appellate courts.
Complaint	The pleading in a civil case in which the plaintiff states his claim and requests relief is called complaint. In the common law, it is a formal legal document that sets out the basic facts and legal reasons that the filing party (the plaintiffs) believes are sufficient to support a claim against another person, persons, entity or entities (the defendants) that entitles the plaintiff(s) to a remedy (either money damages or injunctive relief).
Communication	Communication refers to the social process in which two or more parties exchange information and share meaning.

Chapter 6. MOTIVATING OTHERS

Chapter 7. MANAGING CONFLICT

Management	Management characterizes the process of leading and directing all or part of an organization, often a business, through the deployment and manipulation of resources. Early twentieth-century management writer Mary Parker Follett defined management as "the art of getting things done through people."
Manager	A person who is formally responsible for supporting the work efforts of other people is a manager.
Leading indicator	A leading indicator is an economic indicator which tends to change before the general economic activity.
Globalization	Trend away from distinct national economic units and toward one huge global market is called globalization. Globalization is caused by four fundamental forms of capital movement throughout the global economy.
Workforce diversity	The similarities and differences in such characteristics as age, gender, ethnic heritage, physical abilities and disabilities, race, and sexual orientation among the employees of organizations is called workforce diversity.
Status quo	The existing state of things is the status quo. In contract law, returning a party to status quo or status quo ante means putting him in the position he was in before entering the contract.
Innovation	The process of creating and doing new things that are introduced into the marketplace as products, processes, or services is innovation.
Cultural values	The values that employees need to have and act on for the organization to act on the strategic values are called cultural values.
Holding	The holding is a court's determination of a matter of law based on the issue presented in the particular case. In other words: under this law, with these facts, this result.
Competition	In business, competition occurs when rival organizations with similar products and services attempt to gain customers.
Preference	The act of a debtor in paying or securing one or more of his creditors in a manner more favorable to them than to other creditors or to the exclusion of such other creditors is a preference. In the absence of statute, a preference is perfectly good, but to be legal it must be bona fide, and not a mere subterfuge of the debtor to secure a future benefit to himself or to prevent the application of his property to his debts.
Acceptance	The actual or implied receipt and retention of that which is tendered or offered is the acceptance.
Composition	An out-of-court settlement in which creditors agree to accept a fractional settlement on their original claim is referred to as composition.
Devil's advocate	A decision-making technique in which an individual is assigned the role of challenging the assumptions and assertions made by the group to prevent premature consensus is the devil's advocate.
Competitive advantage	A business is said to have a competitive advantage when its unique strengths, often based on cost, quality, time, and innovation, offer consumers a greater percieved value and there by differtiating it from its competitors.
Interpersonal skills	Interpersonal skills are used to communicate with, understand, and motivate individuals and groups.
Effective manager	Leader of a team that consistently achieves high performance goals is an effective manager.

Go to Cram101.com for the Practice Tests for this Chapter.

Chapter 7. MANAGING CONFLICT

Chapter 7. MANAGING CONFLICT

Remainder	A remainder in property law is a future interest created in a transferee that is capable of becoming possessory upon the natural termination of a prior estate created by the same instrument.
Context	The effect of the background under which a message often takes on more and richer meaning is a context. Context is especially important in cross-cultural interactions because some cultures are said to be high context or low context.
Intervention	A proceeding by which one not originally made a party to an action or suit is permitted, on his own application, to appear therein and join one of the original parties in maintaining his cause of action or defense, or to assert some cause of action against some or all of the parties to the proceeding as originally instituted is an intervention.
Categorizing	The act of placing strengths and weaknesses into categories in generic internal assessment is called categorizing.
Devise	In a will, a gift of real property is called a devise.
Negotiation	Negotiation is the process whereby interested parties resolve disputes, agree upon courses of action, bargain for individual or collective advantage, and/or attempt to craft outcomes which serve their mutual interests.
Accounting	The recording, classifying, summarizing, and interpreting of financial events and transactions to provide management and other interested parties the information they need to make good decisions is called accounting.
Small business	Small business refers to a business that is independently owned and operated, is not dominant in its field of operation, and meets certain standards of size in terms of employees or annual receipts.
Respondent	Respondent refers to a term often used to describe the party charged in an administrative proceeding. The party adverse to the appellant in a case appealed to a higher court.
Content	Content refers to all digital information included on a website, including the presentation form-text, video, audio, and graphics.
Argument	The discussion by counsel for the respective parties of their contentions on the law and the facts of the case being tried in order to aid the jury in arriving at a correct and just conclusion is called argument.
Organizational environment	Organizational environment refers to everything outside an organization. It includes all elements, people, other organizations, economic factors, objects, and events that lie outside the boundaries of the organization.
Equity	Equity is the name given to the set of legal principles, in countries following the English common law tradition, which supplement strict rules of law where their application would operate harshly, so as to achieve what is sometimes referred to as "natural justice."
Interest	Interest refers to the payment the issuer of the bond makes to the bondholders for use of the borrowed money. It is the return to capital achieved over time or as the result of an event.
Strike	A strike is a nonviolent work stoppage for the purpose of obtaining better terms and conditions of employment under a collective bargaining agreement.
Communication	Communication refers to the social process in which two or more parties exchange information and share meaning.
Complexity	The technical sophistication of the product and hence the amount of understanding required to use it is referred to as complexity. It is the opposite of simplicity.
Marketing	The American Marketing Association suggests that Marketing is "the process of planning and

Chapter 7. MANAGING CONFLICT

Chapter 7. MANAGING CONFLICT

	executing the pricing, promotion, and distribution of goods, ideas, and services to create exchanges that satisfy individual and organizational goals."
Production	The creation of finished goods and services using the factors of production: land, labor, capital, entrepreneurship, and knowledge.
Compliance	A type of influence process where a receiver accepts the position advocated by a source to obtain favorable outcomes or to avoid punishment is the compliance.
Efficiency	Efficiency refers to the use of minimal resources, such as raw materials, money, and people- to produce a desired volume of output.
Organizational goals	Objectives that management seeks to achieve in pursuing the firm's purpose are organizational goals.
Product	Any physical good, service, or idea that satisfies a want or need is called product. Product in project management is a physical entity created as a result of project work.
Revenue	Revenue refers to the total amount of money a business earns in a given period by selling goods and services. The value of what is received for goods sold, services rendered.
Mediation	Mediation consists of a process of alternative dispute resolution in which a (generally) neutral third party using appropriate techniques, assists two or more parties to help them negotiate an agreement, with concrete effects, on a matter of common interest.
Budget	A financial plan that sets forth management's expectations for revenues and, based on those expectations, allocates the use of specific resources throughout the firm is called budget.
Ethnocentrism	Ironically, ethnocentrism may be something that all cultures have in common. People often feel this occurring during what some call culture shock. Ethnocentrism often entails the belief that one's own race or ethnic group is the most important and/or that some or all aspects of its culture are superior to those of other groups.
Participation	Participation refers to the process of giving employees a voice in making decisions about their own work.
Trust	Trust refers to a legal relationship in which a person who has legal title to property has the duty to hold it for the use or benefit of another person. The term is also used in a general sense to mean confidence reposed in one person by another.
Downsizing	The process of eliminating managerial and non-managerial positions are called downsizing.
Standing	Standing refers to the legal requirement that anyone seeking to challenge a particular action in court must demonstrate that such action substantially affects his legitimate interests before he will be entitled to bring suit.
Authority	Authority in agency law, refers to an agent's ability to affect his principal's legal relations with third parties. Also used to refer to an actor's legal power or ability to do something. In addition, sometimes used to refer to a statute, case, or other legal source that justifies a particular result.
Joint venture	A form of business organization identical to a partnership, except that it is engaged in a single project, not carrying on a business is called the joint venture.
Industry	Industry refers to a group of firms offering products that are close substitutes for each other.
Interdependence	The extent to which departments depend on each other for resources or materials to accomplish their tasks is referred to as interdependence.
Capital	Contributions of money and other property to a business made by the owners of the business are capital.

Go to Cram101.com for the Practice Tests for this Chapter.

Chapter 7. MANAGING CONFLICT

Chapter 7. MANAGING CONFLICT

Stock	In financial terminology, stock is the capital raized by a corporation, through the issuance and sale of shares. A shareholder is any person or organization which owns one or more shares of a corporation's stock. The aggregate value of a corporation's issued shares is its market capitalization.
Committee	A long-lasting, sometimes permanent team in the organization structure created to deal with tasks that recur regularly is the committee.
Subculture	A subgroups within the larger, or national, culture with unique values, ideas, and attitudes is a subculture.
Personnel	A collective term for all of the employees of an organization. Personnel is also commonly used to refer to the personnel management function or the organizational unit responsible for administering personnel programs.
Cooperative	A business owned and controlled by the people who use it, producers, consumers, or workers with similar needs who pool their resources for mutual gain is called cooperative.
Compromise	Compromise occurs when the interaction is moderately important to meeting goals and the goals are neither completely compatible nor completely incompatible.
Appeal	Appeal refers to the act of asking an appellate court to overturn a decision after the trial court's final judgment has been entered.
Mistake	In contract law a mistake is incorrect understanding by one or more parties to a contract and may be used as grounds to invalidate the agreement. Common law has identified three different types of mistake in contract: unilateral mistake, mutual mistake, and common mistake.
Collaboration	Collaboration occurs when the interaction between groups is very important to goal attainment and the goals are compatible. Wherein people work together —applying both to the work of individuals as well as larger collectives and societies.
Conflict resolution	Conflict resolution is the process of resolving a dispute or a conflict. Successful conflict resolution occurs by providing each side's needs, and adequately addressing their interests so that they are each satisfied with the outcome. Conflict resolution aims to end conflicts before they start or lead to physical fighting.
Entrepreneur	A person who assumes the risk of time and money to start and manage a business is an entrepreneur.
Distributive bargaining	Distributive bargaining is the approach to bargaining or negotiation that is used when the parties are trying to divide something up--distribute something.
Consideration	Consideration in contract law, a basic requirement for an enforceable agreement under traditional contract principles, defined in this text as legal value, bargained for and given in exchange for an act or promise. In corporation law, cash or property contributed to a corporation in exchange for shares, or a promise to contribute such cash or property.
Assessment	Collecting information and providing feedback to employees about their behavior, communication style, or skills is an assessment.
Loyalty	Marketers tend to define customer loyalty as making repeat purchases. Some argue that it should be defined attitudinally as a strongly positive feeling about the brand.
Partnership	In the common law, a partnership is a type of business structure in which partners share with each other the profits or losses of the business undertaking in which they have all invested.
Accommodation	Accommodation is a term used to describe a delivery of nonconforming goods meant as a partial performance of a contract for the sale of goods, where a full performance is not possible.
Brief	Brief refers to a statement of a party's case or legal arguments, usually prepared by an

Chapter 7. MANAGING CONFLICT

Chapter 7. MANGING CONFLICT

	attorney. Also used to make legal arguments before appellate courts.
Competencies	An organization's special capabilities, including skills, technologies, and resources that distinguish it from other organizations are competencies.
Integrative bargaining	The part of the labor-management negotiation process that seeks solutions beneficial to both sides is called integrative bargaining.
Productivity	Productivity refers to the total output of goods and services in a given period of time divided by work hours.
Brainstorming	Brainstorming refers to a technique designed to overcome our natural tendency to evaluate and criticize ideas and thereby reduce the creative output of those ideas. People are encouraged to produce ideas/options without criticizing, often at a very fast pace to minimize our natural tendency to criticize.
Options	Options give the owner the right but not the obligation to buy or sell an underlying security at a set price for a given time period.
Action plan	Action plan refers to a written document that includes the steps the trainee and manager will take to ensure that training transfers to the job.
Exchange	The trade of things of value between buyer and seller so that each is better off after the trade is called the exchange.
Complaint	The pleading in a civil case in which the plaintiff states his claim and requests relief is called complaint. In the common law, it is a formal legal document that sets out the basic facts and legal reasons that the filing party (the plaintiffs) believes are sufficient to support a claim against another person, persons, entity or entities (the defendants) that entitles the plaintiff(s) to a remedy (either money damages or injunctive relief).
Accountability	The extent to which one must answer to higher authority-legal or organizational-for one's actions in society at large or within one's particular organizational position is an accountability.
Principal	In agency law, one under whose direction an agent acts and for whose benefit that agent acts is a principal.
Rebuttal	Testimony addressed to evidence produced by the opposite party is referred to as rebuttal.
Audit	Audit refers to the verification of a company's books and records pursuant to federal securities laws, state laws, and stock exchange rules that must be performed by an independent CPA.
Assault	An intentional tort that prohibits any attempt or offer to cause harmful or offensive contact with another if it results in a well-grounded apprehension of imminent battery in the mind of the threatened person is called assault.
Promotion	Promotion refers to all the techniques sellers use to motivate people to buy products or services. An attempt by marketers to inform people about products and to persuade them to participate in an exchange.
Allegation	An allegation is a statement of a fact by a party in a pleading, which the party claims it will prove. Allegations remain assertions without proof, only claims until they are proved.
Policy	Similar to a script in that a policy can be a less than completely rational decision-making method. Involves the use of a pre-existing set of decision steps for any problem that presents itself.
Warrant	A warrant is a security that entitles the holder to buy or sell a certain additional quantity of an underlying security at an agreed-upon price, at the holder's discretion.

Go to **Cram101.com** for the Practice Tests for this Chapter.

Chapter 7. MANAGING CONFLICT

Chapter 7. MANAGING CONFLICT

Credibility	The extent to which a source is perceived as having knowledge, skill, or experience relevant to a communication topic and can be trusted to give an unbiased opinion or present objective information on the issue is called credibility.
Facilitator	A facilitator is someone who skilfully helps a group of people understand their common objectives and plan to achieve them without personally taking any side of the argument.
Verdict	Usually, the decision made by a jury and reported to the judge on the matters or questions submitted to it at trial is a verdict. In some situations, however, the judge may be the party issuing a verdict.

Chapter 7. MANAGING CONFLICT

Chapter 8. EMPOWERING AND DELEGATING

Management	Management characterizes the process of leading and directing all or part of an organization, often a business, through the deployment and manipulation of resources. Early twentieth-century management writer Mary Parker Follett defined management as "the art of getting things done through people."
Manager	A person who is formally responsible for supporting the work efforts of other people is a manager.
Empowerment	Giving employees the authority and responsibility to respond quickly to customer requests is called empowerment.
Delegation	Delegation is the handing of a task over to another person, usually a subordinate. It is the assignment of authority and responsibility to another person to carry out specific activities.
Incentive	A reward offered by a marketer to a prospective customer in return for furnishing information or making a purchase is referred to as an incentive.
Context	The effect of the background under which a message often takes on more and richer meaning is a context. Context is especially important in cross-cultural interactions because some cultures are said to be high context or low context.
Extrinsic reward	Extrinsic reward refers to something given to you by someone else as recognition for good work; extrinsic rewards include pay increases, praise, and promotions.
Visibility	Visibility is used in marketing, as a measure of how much the public sees a product or its advertising.
Alienation	The voluntary act or acts by which one-person transfers his or her own property to another is referred to as alienation.
Complexity	The technical sophistication of the product and hence the amount of understanding required to use it is referred to as complexity. It is the opposite of simplicity.
Competition	In business, competition occurs when rival organizations with similar products and services attempt to gain customers.
Autocratic leadership	Leadership style that involves making managerial decisions without consulting others is an autocratic leadership.
Accountability	The extent to which one must answer to higher authority-legal or organizational-for one's actions in society at large or within one's particular organizational position is an accountability.
Participation	Participation refers to the process of giving employees a voice in making decisions about their own work.
Downsizing	The process of eliminating managerial and non-managerial positions are called downsizing.
Escalating commitment	The tendency to continue a previously chosen course of action even when feedback suggests that it is failing is an escalating commitment.
Options	Options give the owner the right but not the obligation to buy or sell an underlying security at a set price for a given time period.
Communication	Communication refers to the social process in which two or more parties exchange information and share meaning.
Productivity	Productivity refers to the total output of goods and services in a given period of time divided by work hours.
Trust	Trust refers to a legal relationship in which a person who has legal title to property has

Go to **Cram101.com** for the Practice Tests for this Chapter.

Chapter 8. EMPOWERING AND DELEGATING

Chapter 8. EMPOWERING AND DELEGATING

	the duty to hold it for the use or benefit of another person. The term is also used in a general sense to mean confidence reposed in one person by another.
Loyalty	Marketers tend to define customer loyalty as making repeat purchases. Some argue that it should be defined attitudinally as a strongly positive feeling about the brand.
Hierarchy	A system of grouping people in an organization according to rank from the top down in which all subordinate managers must report to one person is called a hierarchy.
Acquisition	A company's purchase of the property and obligations of another company is an acquisition.
Team building	A term that describes the process of identifying roles for team members and helping the team members succeed in their roles is called team building.
Brief	Brief refers to a statement of a party's case or legal arguments, usually prepared by an attorney. Also used to make legal arguments before appellate courts.
Agency	Agency refers to a legal relationship in which an agent acts under the direction of a principal for the principal's benefit. Also used to refer to government regulatory bodies of all kinds.
Controlling	A management function that involves determining whether or not an organization is progressing toward its goals and objectives, and taking corrective action if it is not is called controlling.
Job enrichment	A motivational strategy that emphasizes motivating the worker through the job itself is called job enrichment.
Self-efficacy	The extent to which we believe we can accomplish our goals even if we failed to do so in the past is referred to as self-efficacy.
Accord	An agreement whereby the parties agree to accept something different in satisfaction of the original contract is an accord.
Alignment	Term that refers to optimal coordination among disparate departments and divisions within a firm is referred to as alignment.
Value system	A value system refers to how an individual or a group of individuals organize their ethical or ideological values. A well-defined value system is a moral code.
Expense	An expense refers to costs involved in operating a business, such as rent, utilities, and salaries.
Efficiency	Efficiency refers to the use of minimal resources, such as raw materials, money, and people- to produce a desired volume of output.
Value-added	A customer-based perspective on quality that is used by services, manufacturing, and public sector organizations is value-added. The concept of value-added involves a subjective assessment of the efficacy of every step in the process for the customer.
Authority	Authority in agency law, refers to an agent's ability to affect his principal's legal relations with third parties. Also used to refer to an actor's legal power or ability to do something. In addition, sometimes used to refer to a statute, case, or other legal source that justifies a particular result.
Holding	The holding is a court's determination of a matter of law based on the issue presented in the particular case. In other words: under this law, with these facts, this result.
Resistance to change	Resistance to change refers to an attitude or behavior that shows unwillingness to make or support a change.
Bureaucracy	Bureaucracy refers to an organization with many layers of managers who set rules and

Chapter 8. EMPOWERING AND DELEGATING

Chapter 8. EMPOWERING AND DELEGATING

	regulations and oversee all decisions.
Formal organization	Formal organization refers to the structure that details lines of responsibility, authority, and position; that is, the structure shown on organization charts.
Committee	A long-lasting, sometimes permanent team in the organization structure created to deal with tasks that recur regularly is the committee.
Task force	A temporary team or committee formed to solve a specific short-term problem involving several departments is the task force.
Corporation	A form of business organization that is owned by owners, called shareholders, who have no inherent right to manage the business, and is managed by a board of directors that is elected by the shareholders is called a corporation.
Mentor	An experienced employee who supervises, coaches, and guides lower-level employees by introducing them to the right people and generally being their organizational sponsor is a mentor.
Competencies	An organization's special capabilities, including skills, technologies, and resources that distinguish it from other organizations are competencies.
Effective manager	Leader of a team that consistently achieves high performance goals is an effective manager.
Human resources	Human resources refers to the individuals within the firm, and to the portion of the firm's organization that deals with hiring, firing, training, and other personnel issues.
Marketing	The American Marketing Association suggests that Marketing is "the process of planning and executing the pricing, promotion, and distribution of goods, ideas, and services to create exchanges that satisfy individual and organizational goals."
Institutional investors	Institutional investors refers to large organizations‹such as pension funds, mutual funds, insurance companies, and banks‹that invest their own funds or the funds of others.
Revenue	Revenue refers to the total amount of money a business earns in a given period by selling goods and services. The value of what is received for goods sold, services rendered.
Privilege	Generally, a legal right to engage in conduct that would otherwise result in legal liability is a privilege. Privileges are commonly classified as absolute or conditional. Occasionally, privilege is also used to denote a legal right to refrain from particular behavior.
Assignment	A transfer of property or some right or interest is referred to as assignment.
Policy	Similar to a script in that a policy can be a less than completely rational decision-making method. Involves the use of a pre-existing set of decision steps for any problem that presents itself.
Possession	Possession refers to respecting real property, exclusive dominion and control such as owners of like property usually exercise over it. Manual control of personal property either as owner or as one having a qualified right in it.
Users	Users refer to people in the organization who actually use the product or service purchased by the buying center.
Confirmed	When the seller's bank agrees to assume liability on the letter of credit issued by the buyer's bank the transaction is confirmed. The term means that the credit is not only backed up by the issuing foreign bank, but that payment is also guaranteed by the notifying American bank.
Complaint	The pleading in a civil case in which the plaintiff states his claim and requests relief is called complaint. In the common law, it is a formal legal document that sets out the basic

Go to **Cram101.com** for the Practice Tests for this Chapter.

Chapter 8. EMPOWERING AND DELEGATING

Chapter 8. EMPOWERING AND DELEGATING

	facts and legal reasons that the filing party (the plaintiffs) believes are sufficient to support a claim against another person, persons, entity or entities (the defendants) that entitles the plaintiff(s) to a remedy (either money damages or injunctive relief).
Exhibit	Exhibit refers to a copy of a written instrument on which a pleading is founded, annexed to the pleading and by reference made a part of it. Any paper or thing offered in evidence and marked for identification.
Mistake	In contract law a mistake is incorrect understanding by one or more parties to a contract and may be used as grounds to invalidate the agreement. Common law has identified three different types of mistake in contract: unilateral mistake, mutual mistake, and common mistake.
Comprehensive	A comprehensive refers to a layout accurate in size, color, scheme, and other necessary details to show how a final ad will look. For presentation only, never for reproduction.
Assessment	Collecting information and providing feedback to employees about their behavior, communication style, or skills is an assessment.
Acceptance	The actual or implied receipt and retention of that which is tendered or offered is the acceptance.
Coordination	Coordination refers to the set of mechanisms used in an organization to link the actions of its subunits into a consistent pattern.
Arbitrate	To submit some disputed matter to selected persons and to accept their decision or award as a substitute for the decision of a judicial tribunal is called the arbitrate.
Content	Content refers to all digital information included on a website, including the presentation form-text, video, audio, and graphics.
Acceptance theory of authority	The theory that the manager's authority depends on the subordinate's acceptance of the manager's right to give directives and to expect compliance with them is called acceptance theory of authority.
Organizational structure	Refers to how a company is put together and reflects some of the underlying ways that people interact with one another in and across jobs or departments is referred to as organizational structure.
Chain of command	An unbroken line of authority that links all individuals in the organization and specifies who reports to whom is a chain of command. The concept of chain of command also implies that higher rank alone does not entitle a person to give commands.
Interest	Interest refers to the payment the issuer of the bond makes to the bondholders for use of the borrowed money. It is the return to capital achieved over time or as the result of an event.
Budget	A financial plan that sets forth management's expectations for revenues and, based on those expectations, allocates the use of specific resources throughout the firm is called budget.
Task performance	The quantity and quality of work produced is referred to as the task performance. Actions taken to ensure that the work group reaches its goals.
Innovation	The process of creating and doing new things that are introduced into the marketplace as products, processes, or services is innovation.
Contribution	In business organization law, the cash or property contributed to a business by its owners is referred to as contribution.

Go to **Cram101.com** for the Practice Tests for this Chapter.

Chapter 8. EMPOWERING AND DELEGATING

Chapter 9. BUILDING EFFECTIVE TEAMS AND TEAMWORK

Teamwork	That which occurs when group members work together in ways that utilize their skills well to accomplish a purpose is called teamwork.
Efficiency	Efficiency refers to the use of minimal resources, such as raw materials, money, and people- to produce a desired volume of output.
Productivity	Productivity refers to the total output of goods and services in a given period of time divided by work hours.
Trust	Trust refers to a legal relationship in which a person who has legal title to property has the duty to hold it for the use or benefit of another person. The term is also used in a general sense to mean confidence reposed in one person by another.
Participation	Participation refers to the process of giving employees a voice in making decisions about their own work.
Advertisement	Advertisement is the promotion of goods, services, companies and ideas, usually by an identified sponsor. Marketers see advertising as part of an overall promotional strategy.
Autonomous work groups	Groups used to integrate an organization's technical and social systems for the benefit of large systems are referred to as autonomous work groups.
Management	Management characterizes the process of leading and directing all or part of an organization, often a business, through the deployment and manipulation of resources. Early twentieth-century management writer Mary Parker Follett defined management as "the art of getting things done through people."
Virtual team	A group of physically dispersed people who work as a team via alternative communication modes is called virtual team.
Quality control	The measurement of products and services against set standards is referred to as quality control.
Interdependence	The extent to which departments depend on each other for resources or materials to accomplish their tasks is referred to as interdependence.
Assessment	Collecting information and providing feedback to employees about their behavior, communication style, or skills is an assessment.
Team building	A term that describes the process of identifying roles for team members and helping the team members succeed in their roles is called team building.
Groupthink	Groupthink is a situation in which pressures for cohesion and togetherness are so strong as to produce narrowly considered and bad decisions; this can be especially true via conformity pressures in groups.
Composition	An out-of-court settlement in which creditors agree to accept a fractional settlement on their original claim is referred to as composition.
Comprehensive	A comprehensive refers to a layout accurate in size, color, scheme, and other necessary details to show how a final ad will look. For presentation only, never for reproduction.
Quality circle	A quality circle is a volunteer group composed of workers who meet together to discuss workplace improvement, and make presentations to management with their ideas.
Communication	Communication refers to the social process in which two or more parties exchange information and share meaning.
Group dynamics	The term group dynamics implies that individual behaviors may differ depending on individuals' current or prospective connections to a sociological group. Group dynamics is the field of study within the social sciences that focuses on the nature of groups. Urges to belong or to identify may make for distinctly different attitudes (recognized or

Chapter 9. BUILDING EFFECTIVE TEAMS AND TEAMWORK

Chapter 9. BUILDING EFFECTIVE TEAMS AND TEAMWORK

	unrecognized), and the influence of a group may rapidly become strong, influencing or overwhelming individual proclivities and actions.
Personnel	A collective term for all of the employees of an organization. Personnel is also commonly used to refer to the personnel management function or the organizational unit responsible for administering personnel programs.
Logistics	Those activities that focus on getting the right amount of the right products to the right place at the right time at the lowest possible cost is referred to as logistics.
Credibility	The extent to which a source is perceived as having knowledge, skill, or experience relevant to a communication topic and can be trusted to give an unbiased opinion or present objective information on the issue is called credibility.
Reciprocity	An industrial buying practice in which two organizations agree to purchase each other's products and services is called reciprocity.
Argument	The discussion by counsel for the respective parties of their contentions on the law and the facts of the case being tried in order to aid the jury in arriving at a correct and just conclusion is called argument.
Status quo	The existing state of things is the status quo. In contract law, returning a party to status quo or status quo ante means putting him in the position he was in before entering the contract.
Controlling	A management function that involves determining whether or not an organization is progressing toward its goals and objectives, and taking corrective action if it is not is called controlling.
Vision statement	The identification of objectives to be achieved in the future is called vision statement.
Puffery	Advertising or other sales presentations that praise the item to be sold using subjective opinions, superlatives, or exaggerations, vaguely and generally, stating no specific facts is called puffery.
Industry	Industry refers to a group of firms offering products that are close substitutes for each other.
Competencies	An organization's special capabilities, including skills, technologies, and resources that distinguish it from other organizations are competencies.
Core	A core is the set of feasible allocations in an economy that cannot be improved upon by subset of the set of the economy's consumers (a coalition).
Exhibit	Exhibit refers to a copy of a written instrument on which a pleading is founded, annexed to the pleading and by reference made a part of it. Any paper or thing offered in evidence and marked for identification.
Manager	A person who is formally responsible for supporting the work efforts of other people is a manager.
Cultural values	The values that employees need to have and act on for the organization to act on the strategic values are called cultural values.
Contribution	In business organization law, the cash or property contributed to a business by its owners is referred to as contribution.
Collaboration	Collaboration occurs when the interaction between groups is very important to goal attainment and the goals are compatible. Wherein people work together —applying both to the work of individuals as well as larger collectives and societies.
Stock	In financial terminology, stock is the capital raized by a corporation, through the issuance

Chapter 9. BUILDING EFFECTIVE TEAMS AND TEAMWORK

Chapter 9. BUILDING EFFECTIVE TEAMS AND TEAMWORK

	and sale of shares. A shareholder is any person or organization which owns one or more shares of a corporation's stock. The aggregate value of a corporation's issued shares is its market capitalization.
Tactic	A short-term immediate decision that, in its totality, leads to the achievement of strategic goals is called a tactic.
Accountability	The extent to which one must answer to higher authority-legal or organizational-for one's actions in society at large or within one's particular organizational position is an accountability.
Facilitator	A facilitator is someone who skilfully helps a group of people understand their common objectives and plan to achieve them without personally taking any side of the argument.
Assignment	A transfer of property or some right or interest is referred to as assignment.
Facilitation	Facilitation refers to helping a team or individual achieve a goal. Often used in meetings or with teams to help the teams achieve their objectives.
Empathy	Empathy refers to dimension of service quality-caring individualized attention provided to customers.
Forming	The first stage of team development, where the team is formed and the objectives for the team are set is referred to as forming.
Receiver	A person that is appointed as a custodian of other people's property by a court of law or a creditor of the owner, pending a lawsuit or reorganization is called a receiver.
Context	The effect of the background under which a message often takes on more and richer meaning is a context. Context is especially important in cross-cultural interactions because some cultures are said to be high context or low context.
Norming	The third stage of team development, where the team becomes a cohesive unit, and interdependence, trust, and cooperation are built is called norming.
Brief	Brief refers to a statement of a party's case or legal arguments, usually prepared by an attorney. Also used to make legal arguments before appellate courts.
Interest	Interest refers to the payment the issuer of the bond makes to the bondholders for use of the borrowed money. It is the return to capital achieved over time or as the result of an event.
Regulation	Regulation refers to restrictions state and federal laws place on business with regard to the conduct of its activities.
Cabinet	The heads of the executive departments of a jurisdiction who report to and advise its chief executive; examples would include the president's cabinet, the governor's cabinet, and the mayor's cabinet.
Preference	The act of a debtor in paying or securing one or more of his creditors in a manner more favorable to them than to other creditors or to the exclusion of such other creditors is a preference. In the absence of statute, a preference is perfectly good, but to be legal it must be bona fide, and not a mere subterfuge of the debtor to secure a future benefit to himself or to prevent the application of his property to his debts.
Devil's advocate	A decision-making technique in which an individual is assigned the role of challenging the assumptions and assertions made by the group to prevent premature consensus is the devil's advocate.
Hierarchy	A system of grouping people in an organization according to rank from the top down in which all subordinate managers must report to one person is called a hierarchy.
Product	Any physical good, service, or idea that satisfies a want or need is called product. Product

Chapter 9. BUILDING EFFECTIVE TEAMS AND TEAMWORK

Chapter 9. BUILDING EFFECTIVE TEAMS AND TEAMWORK

	in project management is a physical entity created as a result of project work.
Coalition	An informal alliance among managers who support a specific goal is called coalition.
Bond	A long-term debt security that is secured by collateral is called a bond.
Competition	In business, competition occurs when rival organizations with similar products and services attempt to gain customers.
Visibility	Visibility is used in marketing, as a measure of how much the public sees a product or its advertising.
Superordinate goal	Superordinate goal refers to an organizational goal that is more important to the well-being of the organization and its members than the more specific goals of interacting parties.
Competitor	Other organizations in the same industry or type of business that provide a good or service to the same set of customers is referred to as a competitor.
Corporation	A form of business organization that is owned by owners, called shareholders, who have no inherent right to manage the business, and is managed by a board of directors that is elected by the shareholders is called a corporation.
Loyalty	Marketers tend to define customer loyalty as making repeat purchases. Some argue that it should be defined attitudinally as a strongly positive feeling about the brand.
Continuous improvement	Constantly improving the way the organization does things so that customer needs can be better satisfied is referred to as continuous improvement.
Trial	An examination before a competent tribunal, according to the law of the land, of the facts or law put in issue in a cause, for the purpose of determining such issue is a trial. When the court hears and determines any issue of fact or law for the purpose of determining the rights of the parties, it may be considered a trial.
Innovation	The process of creating and doing new things that are introduced into the marketplace as products, processes, or services is innovation.
Purchasing	Purchasing refers to the function in a firm that searches for quality material resources, finds the best suppliers, and negotiates the best price for goods and services.

Chapter 9. BUILDING EFFECTIVE TEAMS AND TEAMWORK

Printed in the United States
67698LVS00006B/31